Cognitive Psychology

KNOWLEDGE IN A NUTSHELL

Cognitive Psychology

KNOWLEDGE
IN A
NUTSHELL

Shona Saul

SIRIUS

SIRIUS

This edition published in 2025 by Sirius Publishing, a division of
Arcturus Publishing Limited,
26/27 Bickels Yard, 151–153 Bermondsey Street,
London SE1 3HA

ISBN. 978-1-3988-4358-5
AD010858UK

Printed in China

Contents

Chapter 1

Introduction

WHAT IS COGNITIVE PSYCHOLOGY?

Let's imagine that you've decided to make yourself a cup of tea to enjoy while reading a magazine, the day's news or a book. Part of the reason for engaging in both activities together is that you think doing so will be time-saving. You fill the kettle, locate the box of teabags, some milk and a mug. Once the tea is prepared, you get your magazine, newspaper, mobile phone or book and start to read and look at the associated photographs.

Nothing that you have done is out of the ordinary. All your behaviours are so commonplace that they really don't stand out unless something goes wrong, such as forgetting to switch on the kettle, misreading one word as another, or failing to recognize a photograph of someone famous. That these behaviours typically occur so very smoothly contributes to the effective running of our daily lives. Put simply, we can rely on our being able to *just get on with things*. Yet, it is precisely because of this that the mental activities that underpin such daily behaviours are extremely important.

Linking this to our scenario, ***problem solving and decision making*** skills were used in organizing your time efficiently. ***Perception, memory*** and previous ***learning*** were part of identifying the items needed for tea making and following its preparation stages. While reading, marks on a page had to be perceived and identified and then translated into meaning using *language* and memory processes. *Attention* had to be given to the tasks too, while *emotion* can influence mental processes such as attention, perception, memory, learning and decision making. Finally, *consciousness* is involved in perception and the actions we take in response to incoming information. The words in bold are all topics studied by cognitive psychologists.

PSYCHOLOGY AND COGNITIVE PSYCHOLOGY

Psychology is a broad discipline, covering a variety of areas beyond cognitive topics.

An indication of its range is provided in the table opposite. It should be noted that although each area is identified separately, where appropriate one field draws upon another, such that there exists a great deal of interaction across psychology's different specialisms. This certainly applies with cognitive psychology, where its topics also appear in developmental, social, clinical, educational and forensic psychology, for instance. Let us look at this from the perspective of *memory*, which, in addition to being a major topic in cognitive psychology, also contributes significantly to essential understanding elsewhere within the discipline.

Memory is affected in dementia, which comes under the remit of clinical psychology; it is also affected by neurological issues, such as a stroke, covered in the field of neuropsychology. Problems with memory can impact learning in children, which involves developmental psychology and educational psychology. Eyewitnesses to crime are central to investigations, and those factors that influence eyewitness-memory are considered within forensic psychology.

A BRIEF HISTORY OF COGNITIVE PSYCHOLOGY

Cognitive psychology's earliest roots can be traced to the philosophers of Ancient Greece. Aristotle (384–322 BCE), for example, had an interest in issues such as perception and memory. He

PSYCHOLOGY TYPE	BRIEF DESCRIPTION
Biopsychology	biological factors, e.g. the nervous system (including the brain), hormones, heredity.
Cognitive psychology	mental processes such as perception, attention, memory, language, problem solving, reasoning, consciousness and emotion.
Developmental psychology	biological, cognitive, social and emotional change over life.
Social psychology	behaviour in a social context, e.g. relationships, obedience, prejudice.
Individual differences	differences between people, e.g. personality, intelligence.
Evolutionary and comparative psychology	evolutionary theory is applied to explain behaviour; similarities/differences are compared between different species to understand evolutionary relationships.
Clinical psychology	helps with mental and/or physical health issues, e.g. depression, addiction.
Neuropsychology	helps those with a brain injury, tumour, stroke, neurodegenerative disease, toxic and metabolic disorder.
Health psychology	helps those who are physically ill, promotes health and wellbeing and improves healthcare systems.

Counselling psychology	helps with mental health difficulties arising from life circumstances, e.g. bereavement, domestic violence.
Educational psychology	helps children and young people with, for example, learning, social and emotional difficulties.
Occupational psychology	helps improve job satisfaction and the effectiveness of organizations/corporations.
Forensic psychology	psychology is used regarding issues such as criminal investigations, psychological issues and crime, rehabilitation of offenders.
Sport/exercise psychology	sport psychology helps with sports roles, e.g. with training and competition; exercise psychology helps assisting people with regard to exercise, e.g. taking up and maintaining exercise.

conceived perception to consist of *special senses, incidental perception* and *common sensibles*. The special senses (vision, hearing, smell, taste, touch), Aristotle argued, always correctly identify what they sense. Incidental perception, though, involves making a judgement about sensory information, and this may be either correct or incorrect. In this way, if you identify a drink as sour-tasting, you will be right about its sourness but the judgement as to what made it sour may be accurate or inaccurate. Common sensibles, on the other hand, can be perceived by more than one sense. For instance, if seeking a spoon in the kitchen, different kinds of spoon (metal, wooden, large, small, etc.) can be identified by both sight and touch.

For centuries, psychology remained part of philosophy. In 1879, it became an independent discipline in its own right when Wilhelm Wundt established the first psychological laboratory. In the previous year, Hermann Ebbinghaus had begun the first systematic investigations of memory with experimental work which explored how memories are formed and how forgetting occurs. His conclusions were published in *On Memory* (1885). By 1890, William James's classic text *The Principles of Psychology* had appeared, including chapters on topics such as attention, memory, perception and reasoning. In Russia, in the 1890s, Ivan Pavlov was reporting on learning through association: a process known as classical conditioning. Another form of conditioning, operant conditioning, was proposed by B.F. Skinner in the late 1930s. It was based on Edward Thorndike's *Law of Effect* (1898) and proposed that rewarded or reinforced behaviour tends to be repeated.

During the early part of the 20th century, the Gestalt psychologists, Max Wertheimer, Kurt Koffka and Wolfgang Köhler explored the way in which we perceived objects as unified wholes against a stable background. Later, in 1932, Sir Frederic Bartlett published on the reconstructive nature of memory in *Remembering: A Study in Experimental and Social Psychology*.

Cognitive psychology's modern form, though, began to emerge in the 1950s, the decade that gave birth to the information processing approach. During this time, Donald Broadbent discussed how information gleaned by the perceptual system progressed into memory if it received attention. George Miller reported on the capacity of short-term memory; Allen Newell and Herbert Simon developed computer programs which could solve problems in a way which resembled a human's performance, and Noam Chomsky introduced important concepts relating to language. By the end of the 1960s, research had increased significantly and Ulric Neisser published his book, *Cognitive Psychology* (1967), which collected together the latest information on attention, memory, perception, pattern recognition and problem solving.

In 1968, Richard C. Atkinson and Richard M. Shiffrin proposed their model of memory consisting of sensory, short-term and long-term stores. Yet, by 1974, Alan Baddeley and Graham Hitch had begun to describe our current understanding of short-term memory in their *Working Memory Model*. The 1970s and 1980s saw the knowledge base of cognitive psychology expand, through ideas such as Irving Biederman's *Recognition by Components Theory* of 1987, which explored how we perceive and recognize objects. Furthermore, as knowledge concerning brain injury and cognitive impairment grew, cognitive models had to incorporate this too, along with information drawn from research concerning the anatomy and function of neurologically intact brains. This can be seen in Andy Young and Vicki Bruce's 1986 model of face processing, for example. Computer models changed too: connectionist models appeared, such as James McClelland and David Rumelhart's *Interactive Activation Model of Context Effects in Letter Perception* (1981) and Mike Burton and colleagues' interactive activation model of face recognition (1990).

Over time, another change also occurred in cognitive psychology, in terms of whether research studies possessed *ecological validity*. That is, questions were asked about the extent to which traditional research properly reflected and applied to everyday life. More specifically, this related to whether a study's design represented the kinds of natural situations found in daily life, and whether its results could be generalized to real-life situations. Consequently, in the second half of the 20th century, greater research focus was applied to addressing cognitive issues as they appear in day-to-day life.

THIS BOOK

From the sections above, the reader is now aware that cognitive psychology consists of a number of topics; that it uses computer models of cognitive abilities and that it draws upon neurological evidence. The latter includes information on those abilities which are present or absent subsequent to brain damage, plus knowledge gained from techniques which allow *temporal* and *spatial* exploration of the brain. In other words, techniques which indicate when and where a cognitive process is taking place. Examples of these include Positron Emission Tomography, or PET scanning; functional Magnetic Resonance Imaging, or fMRI; and Magneto-Encephalography, or MEG. Last, but by no means least, cognitive psychology has made and continues to make extensive use of experiments designed to explore specific cognitive processes.

Collectively, this means that there is a great deal of material upon which to draw and very little space for discussion! However, the reader should gain a flavour of what cognitive psychology is, within the context of using cognitive abilities in daily life. Let's begin.

Chapter 2

Perception

There are a number of ways in which we sense information. Commonly, we think in terms of the five traditional senses: smell, taste, touch, hearing and sight. Vision involves approximately one third of the human brain, and over 30 areas of the cerebral cortex are associated with visual perception. (The cerebral cortex is the brain's outermost layer and is responsible for our higher-level processes.) This chapter, therefore, focuses upon visual perception and how we recognize both the objects in our environment and the faces of people we encounter.

Initially, though, what is the difference between visual sensation and visual perception? The former results from electrochemical changes which occur as *neurons* (nerve cells) that respond to information in our visual environment. Visual perception involves applying meaning to visual sensation.

SEEING: THE VISUAL SYSTEM

Please consider the material in the box before proceeding further.

> If you are sighted, please complete the following task. If you are blind, or partially-sighted, please still consider the material.
> Take a moment to look around you. What do you see? Perhaps you are seeing green grass, trees, buildings, cars, or

people and their faces? Along with their associated shapes, are you also able to determine if the components of your environment are large or small, stationary or moving?

Seeing begins with light striking the surfaces, edges and textures of what is in our visual environment. Light has different levels of brightness and different wavelengths. To simplify, let's suppose that there is just one object in our visual environment: a tree. Light will hit its trunk, branches and leaves; to see the tree, the light information must be converted into activity in the nerve cells of the visual system.

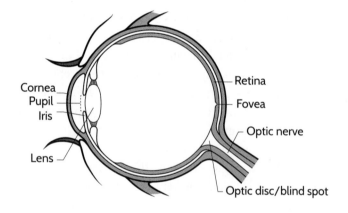

Anatomy of the eye.

Initially, light passes through the transparent, curved *cornea* and then to the *pupil/iris*. The iris is the coloured part of the eye, while the pupil is the black opening in the iris. Muscles connected to the iris regulate the pupil's size. If light is bright, the muscles constrict, making the pupil smaller and thereby limiting how much light enters the eye. When light is low, the muscles relax, enlarging the pupil's size so that more light can enter.

Next, light passes through the curved *lens*. The curvature of the cornea and lens means that light is bent to produce an in-focus image on the retina, at the back of the eye. Muscles attached to the lens allow it to increase and decrease its curvature. Less lens curvature is needed to focus a far object on the retina whereas greater curvature is required to focus a near object.

The retina is the eye's light-sensitive lining and it possesses a small depression in its centre called the *fovea*. When you look at objects in the environment, they are foveated; that is, the light from those objects is focused on to the fovea. The retina possesses a number of different types of cell, but it is the rod and cone cells which convert light into nerve signals that are sent to the brain. Cones function best in bright light, are sensitive to detail and are involved in colour perception. Rods have greater sensitivity to light and so help us to see in low light conditions, along with assisting us to perceive movement in peripheral vision.

MORE ABOUT THE VISUAL IMAGE AT THE RETINA
Once light has travelled through the lens of the eye, the image of what we are looking at is inverted on the retina.

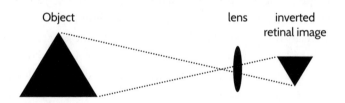

However, this is corrected in the brain, so that what has been seen is perceived as being the correct way up, rather than upside-down. The image at the retina is also two-dimensional, yet we perceive our environment as three-dimensional.

In the fovea there are only cones. In the rest of the retina, beyond the fovea, cones progressively reduce while rods progressively increase. The density of cones at the fovea means that this part of the retina possesses the best acuity, or sharpness/clarity of vision.

Finally, the optic nerve takes retinal information to the brain, initially arriving in a region called the primary visual cortex, at the back of the brain. From here, information is passed to the other areas of the brain also involved in visual processing.

MORE ABOUT THE RETINA AND THE OPTIC NERVE: THE OPTIC DISC AND THE BLIND SPOT

The retina and optic nerve meet at the optic disc. This part of the retina lacks light sensitive cells, which means that, anatomically, there is a blind spot. However, when we look at our environment, we do not experience a patch of missing visual information. Instead, the brain 'fills in' what is missing using information from the other eye.

COLOUR

According to the *Trichromatic Theory* of colour, our sensation of colour results from the retina having three different types of cone: red, green and blue. More precisely, one kind of cone is particularly sensitive to light with a long wavelength, which is perceived as orange-red; another is especially sensitive to medium wavelength light, perceived as yellow-green; the third type of cone responds most to shortwave light, which is perceived as blue. All colours can be detected by combining the relative activity of the three sorts of cone.

However, a problem for the Trichromatic Theory is that it doesn't explain why we experience afterimages of a different colour from the original stimulus. That is, if you were to stare at a green rectangle for roughly half a minute and then looked at a white sheet of paper, you would see a red afterimage. Similarly, if the procedure were repeated with the original rectangle being red, its afterimage would be green. Likewise, a blue rectangle's afterimage would be yellow and a yellow rectangle's afterimage blue. Monochrome afterimages can be produced too with black and white rectangles plus white and black sheets of paper respectively.

The Opponent Process Theory, on the other hand, can explain these phenomena. It contends that the visual system has three pairs of processes for colour: blue-yellow, red-green and black-white. Each of these processes works in opposition. If the blue-yellow process responds in one way yellow will be perceived, but if it responds the opposing way blue will be perceived. Similarly, one kind of response leads to the perception of red and the opposing response to green. With the final pair, either black or white is perceived in like fashion. As a result of pair members opposing each other, when you stare at a green rectangle for half a minute – and all that time the red-green process is signalling green – when you shift your gaze to the white paper, the process now shifts to activating the other member of the red-green pair. Consequently, you see the red afterimage.

The Opponent Process Theory's success at accounting for afterimages does not mean that the Trichromatic Theory is incorrect. Instead, a combination of both theories best explains how we see colour. The Trichromatic Theory accounts for the way in which we can see different colours through our having three kinds of cone, but our cones relay information on to another kind of cell – opponent cells – the activity of which accounts for afterimages.

DEPTH, SIZE CONSTANCY AND SHAPE CONSTANCY

Depth or distance can be determined using *monocular cues, binocular cues* and *oculomotor cues* (see box). With the former, depth can be detected if only one eye is used but both eyes are required for binocular cues. Examples of monocular depth cues can be found in photographs A and B on pages 20 and 22 respectively.

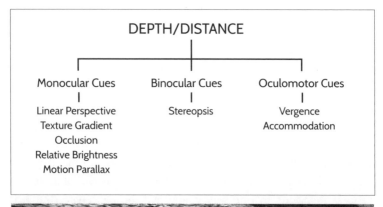

Photograph A, texture gradient: the greater texture detail of the cobblestones in the foreground signals that they are near to the viewer. As the cobblestones decrease in texture detail, this signals that they are at an increasing distance from the viewer.

Linear perspective produced by converging parallel lines signals depth as the horizontal separation between the lines is larger closer to the viewer than it is further away. This can be seen well in photograph B: the lines of houses, vehicles and snow on each side of the street appear to converge as we look further away from the viewing point. *Texture gradient* indicates depth due to there being greater texture detail close to the viewer, which diminishes with distance. In photograph A, the detail of the cobblestones can be clearly seen in the foreground, but it is much harder to identify individual stones as we look along the road. Similarly, in B, where vehicles have left behind two lines of disturbed snow, marks in the snow are present close to the viewer but further away the same lines are smoother.

In B, the vehicles parked on each side of the street obscure or overlap other vehicles and road items: for example, the first car on the left overlaps part of the object behind. This demonstrates the monocular depth cue of *occlusion* – the overlapped object is perceived as being further away. *Relative brightness* can be seen in A; the cobbles in the foreground appear brighter than the more distant stones.

Finally, *motion parallax* involves the viewer moving. Have you ever looked out of the passenger window of a car while being driven and noticed that near objects such as fence posts appear to move quickly, whereas objects further away seem to move very slowly or not at all? Your movement produces position changes and the speed at which the different objects cross the retina is used to assess their distance.

Binocular disparity refers to each eye having a slightly different view. *Stereopsis* is the perception of depth based on binocular disparity. To experience binocular disparity, open and close each eye alternately whilst looking at a close-by object. Having established the disparity between your two eyes, repeat the procedure while looking into the distance. You should find the disparity is greater with closer objects than those at a distance.

Photograph B, linear perspective: the lines of houses, vehicles and snow appear far apart at the point from which the photograph was taken but appear to converge as you look along the street. The convergence of the lines signals increasing depth, or distance, from the viewer.

Turning now to oculomotor cues, *vergence* is a depth cue which draws on the need to contract muscles on either side of each eye in order to focus an object on the fovea. The angle which the eyes must turn inward to foveate a closer object is greater than that required to foveate an object at a greater distance. Our perception of how the muscles have contracted signals depth.

Accommodation refers to the way in which the eye's lens changes shape according to whether an object is near or more distant. Muscles controlling the lens increase its convexity and thickness to focus on near objects and reduce its convexity and thickness to focus on far objects.

With regard to *size* and *shape constancy*, the former captures the way in which the perceptual system allows for increased or decreased distance when perceiving size. In the figure below, a person is approaching a tree in a park. When at position A, the individual is some distance from the tree but at position B is much closer. The retinal image produced by the tree in situation A will be smaller than the one it produces in B, yet the person will not perceive the tree as having enlarged but as having maintained the same size.

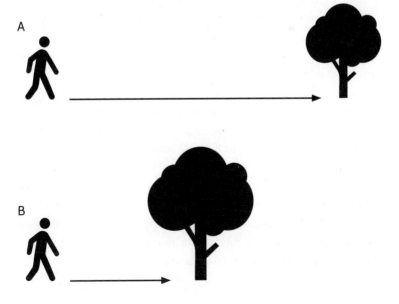

In contrast, shape constancy refers to the way in which an object is perceived to possess a constant shape even when there are changes to its retinal image shape. For example, below is a picture of a British one pound coin from the reign of Queen Elizabeth II. As the coin turns from one image to the next its retinal image changes but we perceive it as maintaining its shape.

Shape constancy: although the coin's retinal image shape changes from one image to the next, its shape is perceived as constant.

ORGANIZING PERCEPTION

When, as requested earlier, you looked about you and observed your environment, it is likely that you saw a number of objects at different distances. Certain objects would have been in front of others and some behind; if you looked out of a window, there may also have been moving vehicles or people, and light would have bounced off all of these objects with their various edges, surfaces and textures. Yet, despite the complex nature of what you saw, you nevertheless perceived an ordered environment in which there were specific objects against a stable background.

An early account of the way in which we perceive our environment as consisting of whole objects against a stable background came from the Gestalt psychologists, in the first half of the 19th century. The Gestalt approach contended that we organize what we see into whole objects by grouping together the individual pieces of visual information we have before us. To experience this, when you look at the figure above right…

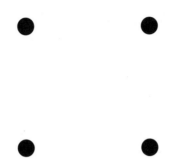

do you perceive the information as four, separate dots, or as a square?

The Gestalt psychologists proposed that we make an important distinction between *figure* (a defined shape) and *ground* (the less important, remaining area which constitutes the background). If you look at the images below, you will readily detect a white arrow on a black background followed by a black triangle on a white background.

Among other characteristics, figures tend to occupy a smaller area than the background, as can be readily observed with the arrow and the triangle. However, what do you see in the above figure, a visual illusion devised by Edgar Rubin?

One option is to interpret the image as a white vase on a black background, or, alternatively, as two profile faces, in black, on a white background. Note, you do not perceive both options simultaneously but must switch between the portions that constitute figure and ground.

There are several Gestalt laws of perceptual organization; *proximity, similarity, good continuation* and *closure* are discussed here:

The Rubin's Jar Illusion.

Proximity

Nearby stimuli tend to be organized into units; on the left, the arrangement of the eight **a** symbols leads them to be perceived as two columns, whereas on the right they appear as two rows.

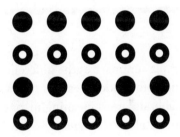

Similarity

Similarity between elements leads them to be grouped together, so that below we perceive rows of dots and rows of doughnuts.

Good Continuation

Elements which flow smoothly from one to the other are organized into units. Here, we perceive two flowing lines.

Closure
A gap in the item is perceptually completed. We perceive the image below as a square despite it being incomplete.

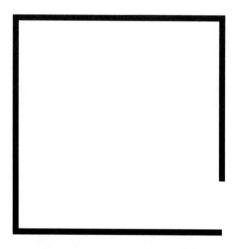

The *Law of Prägnanz* summarizes the different ways in which we organize our visual information. It states that we will perceive the simplest, most stable and most meaningful, or best shape that the visual circumstances allow. (*Prägnanz* is the German word for conciseness or orderliness.)

However, subsequent work by Stephen Palmer and Irvin Rock has indicated that perceptual organization occurs even before we employ Gestalt laws. They proposed the concept of *uniform connectedness*. This means that when we are looking at something which has a connected region in which there is consistent visual information concerning texture, luminance, colour and motion, it is treated as a single perceptual unit. Such single units constitute the first level of visual organization.

RECOGNIZING
Look at images i–iii right: do you recognize them?

(i)

(ii)

(iii)

The first image is, of course, one of the letters of the alphabet written as a capital; (ii) is a book and (iii) the face of Marilyn Monroe. You may have found responding to i–iii very easy, but have you ever asked yourself how you recognize the 26 letters of the alphabet, the various and many objects you encounter in daily life plus all those faces you know personally, or from films, television and other media?

RECOGNIZING PATTERNS AND OBJECTS

Template theory was an early attempt to account for how we recognize stimuli in our environment such as letters and objects. This proposed that we have patterns or *templates* stored in memory against which we compare the current stimulus. Thus, if we are presented with P, for instance, we check this against our stored templates and when the letter we have been presented with matches the P-template, we recognize the stimulus as the letter P.

However, this account is quickly unsatisfactory. Imagine that the P-template looks like this: P. How well would this template overlay each member of the following small selection of possible versions of the letter?

If the P-template cannot cope with all of just 16 variations, how successful would it be with other available fonts plus the various handwritten versions of the letter that can exist? Of course, if there were multiple P-templates, this would increase the occasions when templates would overlay different versions of the letter. Yet, this proposal is not problem-free either. If P has several templates, then this must also apply to the alphabet's other 25 letters. Furthermore, if we expand the theory to include the digits 0–9, because these are the components of all numbers, we would have to hold very many templates in memory to achieve the kind of success we have in recognizing letters and digits, and this hardly seems the most efficient way of operating.

Template Theory's failings led to feature-analysis accounts which proposed that recognition proceeds in terms of

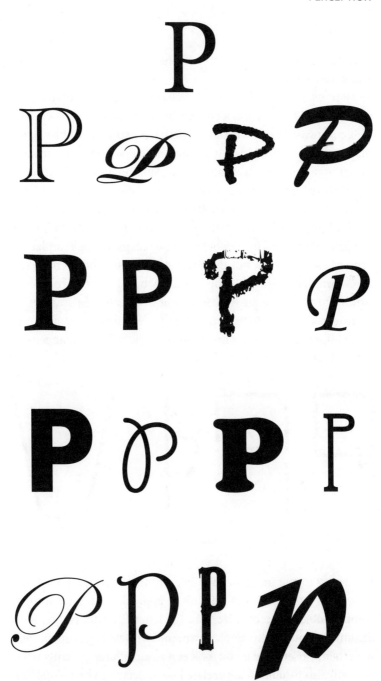

The P-template followed by 16 different versions of the capital letter 'P'.

objects possessing distinctive features, or properties, which characterize them.

For example, a P could be characterized as possessing a straight vertical line; and a curve which contacts the vertical line. This contrasts sharply with an A which has a straight, right-sloping diagonal line, a straight, left-sloping diagonal line and a straight horizontal line which contacts the sloping lines. However, a problem for this theory is that characteristic features may leave a letter unrecognized, or another stimulus which is not a letter recognized as such. For example, when you look at the following, the first two stimuli in (i) would not be recognized as P under the properties described, but the third stimulus fits those characteristics. Similarly, (ii) is clearly not an A but it has the characteristics said to define an A. These issues indicate that features by themselves are insufficient to allow for accurate recognition as extra information is required relating to the relative arrangement of the different properties of a letter.

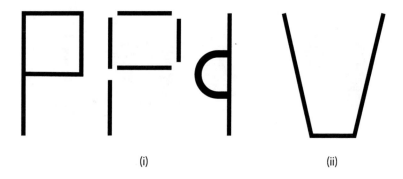

(i)   (ii)

Returning to the images at the beginning of this section, if you look at the book, it is not difficult to appreciate that it is a more complex object to recognize than the letter P. Furthermore, if, in a moment, you set this book down, first with its pages open, then with them closed, and if you look at it from different perspectives, you will also be able to appreciate how objects can be recognized from different perspectives, as also shown on the right.

In the first image, we recognize each object as a book even though individually they are quite different, while in the second image we can recognize the objects as books from their spines alone. In the third picture, we still recognize the objects as books, albeit there is only partial visual information about the objects. Additionally, objects appear differently according to whether they, or we, are moving: for instance, the same car's features change if we look at it head-on, from the side or from the rear.

A feature-detection model would require us to assess whether our object has the appropriately arranged characteristic features of a book or a car for it to be recognized as a *book* or a *car*. Yet, given that objects can be recognized without the presence of salient features – books typically have pages but these are not always visible when we look at a book's spine; half of a car might be hidden by a building and movement could cause feature distortion – more sophisticated approaches to three-dimensional object recognition are required.

These can be found in the work of David Marr, Keith Nishihara and Irving Biederman. Following the proposals of the first two authors, there are three hierarchical stages in object recognition:

1. The *primal sketch*
2. The *2½-D sketch*
3. The *3-D model representation*

Each stage involves creating a representation of objects. The 2½-D sketch uses information from the primal sketch and the 3-D model representation uses information from the 2½-D sketch. As the hierarchy is progressed through, the representation of visual information increases and becomes more detailed.

The primal sketch stage is divided into the *raw primal sketch* and the *full primal sketch*. The raw primal sketch involves the detection of light intensity changes and information about geometric structures such as their size and distance from one to the other. This results in groupings which establish the arrangement, or structural organization, of the scene. Next, the full primal sketch detects how many objects are present and their basic shape using information about edges, texture and contrast differences in what is light versus what is dark.

The 2½-D sketch consists of creating a *viewer-centred* representation of the visual scene. This means that an object's representation consists only of information present in the retinal image, such that the orientation and depth of visible surfaces are represented as they appear from the viewpoint of the individual looking at the object.

As its name implies, at the 3-D model stage an object is represented in three dimensions, its representation shifting from being viewer-centred to *object-centred*. In other words, the viewer now has a representation which is not solely dependent on what can be detected from their viewing position. Instead, the viewer can mentally manipulate the object so that it can be considered from alternative perspectives from the one actually seen. In this way, recognition can go ahead without the necessity of multiple viewer-centred descriptions having to be stored in memory for different objects.

Once the 3-D model has been established from looking at an object, recognition finally occurs when this representation matches with a 3-D model representation held in a catalogue of 3-D models stored in memory.

Turning now to Biederman's *Recognition by Components Theory*, this is a kind of feature detection and integration account of object recognition, in which objects are said to consist of easily distinguishable shapes. These shapes, or *geons* (geometric ions), constitute the units from which we build up the properties of an object. There are approximately 36 geons available to capture an object's characteristics and they include shapes such as cylinders, blocks, wedges, arcs, cones and spheres. To give a simple illustration of this, look at the picture overleaf:

This mug consists of two geons: a cylinder and an arc. The cylinder is the mug's body and the arc its handle.

This object can be built up from two geons: the mug consists of a body, or cylinder, attached to which is its handle, or arc. More complex objects than a mug will consist of more geons; some of these shapes may repeat – for example, there could be more than one block shape – while others could be different.

How, though, do we establish an object's geons?

Firstly, the edges of an object are established using information about colour, brightness and texture. When this information has been extracted, it is used to create a line drawing description of an object, such as our mug. Subsequently, the object is divided up into its different parts using information about which areas are concave. At the same time as this is occurring, the 'nonaccidental' properties of the object are detected.

Some of the edge information we obtain from an object is 'accidental' and some of it is 'nonaccidental'. Accidental information arises from the viewer's specific perspective of an object. Nonaccidental information, on the other hand, involves features which do not change, or are invariant across different viewpoints. Where features are invariant, this means that what is in our two-dimensional visual image is consistent with what is present in the viewed object. The five invariant properties are:

- *Curvature* – an object's curves
- *Parallelism* – an object's parallel lines
- *Cotermination* – edges which terminate at the same point
- *Symmetry* – symmetricity about an axis as opposed to asymmetry
- *Collinearity* – an object's straight lines

Invariant properties do not change as an object's orientation changes, nor are they affected by whether the object is partially hidden.

Once an object's concave regions and nonaccidental properties have been established, its geons can now be determined. Thus, in the case of the photograph of the mug, its geons are identified as a cylinder and an arc.

The penultimate stage of object recognition involves the object's geons and their relationships being matched with its representation in memory. In the case of the mug, when there is a match between its determined components and its structural representation in memory, recognition occurs. Finally, the object is identified; in our example, as a mug.

The last two theories discussed are significant advances on previous accounts of object recognition, but they are not without their own problems. To provide the reader with simple examples of these points: compared with early explanations, Marr, Nishihara and Biederman have provided more detailed and sophisticated theories than those forwarded before. Yet, one limitation shared by both sets of proposals is that while they account for our recognition of different objects – tree, book, car, mug, etc. – they do not explain how we recognize a particular example of an object.

RECOGNIZING FACES

Face recognition, unlike object recognition, requires frequent recognition of *specific examples* of this one kind of visual stimulus. Whereas with objects we often distinguish between different categories of objects, faces belong to the single category 'face', and we must regularly recognize specific individuals from within this category.

Differentiating between different faces is a significant psychological ability because it is the most frequently used route for determining whether a person is known to us or not. Think about how uncomfortable we feel when the process doesn't function correctly and we 'blank' somebody we know, or possibly worse still, greet someone warmly, only to discover the individual is actually a stranger! A face is also very informative about mood. Irrespective of whether the face belongs to our best friend or to someone completely unknown, its facial expression is indicative of a person's emotional state – such as happy, angry, afraid and so forth – and we use this information to inform our own behaviour.

Although a number of different models of face recognition have been proposed, the one which had the greatest impact was devised by Vicki Bruce and Andy Young (see below).

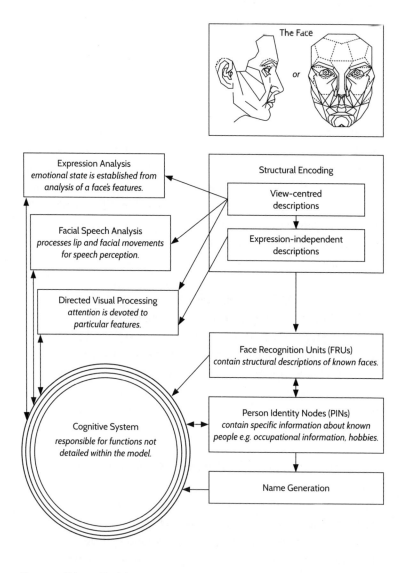

Bruce and Young Model.

Given the model's complexity, an exhaustive consideration is not provided here, rather, an idea of what is involved is provided.

That familiar and unfamiliar faces are dealt with differently is captured in that those modules labelled *face recognition units*, *person identity nodes* and *name generation* are used only in association with familiar faces.

Initially when any face is seen, visual descriptions of it are created (*structural encoding*). However, if the face is familiar, it will possess a face recognition unit because every face that is known has its own face recognition unit, or FRU. An FRU stores a structural description of the face to which it belongs in the form of *structural codes*. When we see a familiar face, the appropriate FRU gives a graded response according to the fit between its stored information and the seen face's description created by structural encoding. This signal is then sent to the cognitive system. Recognition of the face as 'known' follows from there, being a graded response sufficient to signal this level of familiarity.

FACE RECOGNITION PROBLEMS

Failure to Recognize a Familiar Face: there is an insufficient match between the visual descriptions created by structural encoding and the face's stored description within its FRU. This can happen if a person's facial appearance has changed sufficiently so that the FRU possesses out-of-date information, such as when a man grows or shaves off a beard.

Misrecognition of an Unfamiliar Face as Familiar: in this case, the visual descriptions created to an unfamiliar face match sufficiently well with what is stored in a familiar face's FRU, for that FRU to respond, and a signal to be sent to the cognitive system. The FRU's graded signal is sufficient for the unknown face to be deemed – wrongly – as known.

After the FRU stage, information is accessed that allows *person recognition* to occur; that is, we access information specific to the individual concerned. This may be as simple as just 'actor' or 'politician' etc., but could include more specific occupational information (e.g., where the person works), or other information such as where the person lives, or their interests when this information is known. This kind of information is accessed from the activation of a *person identity node* and each known person has their own person identity node, or PIN. (PINs can also be accessed from sources other than the face, such as the person's voice, clothing and gait.) Finally, having accessed the appropriate PIN, the perceived face's name can be produced via *name generation*.

Once a familiar or unfamiliar face has been structurally encoded, it can be assessed for emotional state from analysis of its features (*expression analysis*). Additionally, while a person is speaking, speech perception is assisted via analysis of the face's movements, particularly its lip movements (*facial speech analysis*). *Directed visual processing* involves devoting attention to certain aspects of the face. For example, if we need to remember a new face, we may pay attention to the facial features which will help us recognize it in the future, such as a cleft chin, button nose, or broad forehead. Similarly, if a friend possesses these features and we need to be able to recognize them among a crowd, we can look for faces which possess the relevant features.

THE MCGURK ILLUSION:
FUSING VISUAL AND AUDITORY INFORMATION
In the 1970s, Harry McGurk and John MacDonald reported research in which people were shown a film. Only a woman's head could be seen and the auditory information that could be heard was the woman repeatedly saying the same one syllable, 'ba'. However, 'ba' had been dubbed on to her lip movements which were articulating a different single syllable: 'ga'. What people reported hearing was neither 'ba' nor 'ga'; instead, they said that they heard 'da', a fusion of the

two simultaneously presented syllables. Additionally, when people heard 'ba' without seeing the film, they reported having heard 'ba'. Similarly, when they saw 'ga' without any auditory input, they reported 'ga'. This demonstrates that speech perception is contributed to by lip movements.

A smiling baby. Happiness is just one of the emotions we can detect from a face by analyzing its features.

Finally, the cognitive system is responsible for those functions not detailed within the model. These include taking decisions, initiating responses, directing attention to other parts of the model and holding or accessing specific information that is not held by the person identity nodes, such as a particular film in which an actor has appeared. For instance, when looking at the photograph of Marilyn Monroe, it may have been possible to recognize her face as familiar, identify her as a female actor and name her as *Marilyn Monroe* but also fail to recall the name of the film in which she starred with Jack Lemmon and Tony Curtis. The cognitive system would assist with the associated memory of the movie's title: *Some Like It Hot*.

Twenty-five years after proposing their model, Young and Bruce had the opportunity to review it in the light of research that had taken place in the interim. This led to their discussing a number of issues regarding their original model, of which two will be mentioned here. Young and Bruce noted that they did not include gaze perception within their model. One reason why the addition of gaze information is important is because it provides information as to the subject of a person's attention. A second problem exists with the *expression analysis* module, because it was proposed as a single system. Evidence has now revealed that this cannot be so: damage to different brain areas leads to different emotion-recognition impairments. One kind of damage can lead to problems recognizing fear and anger, while other damage can produce difficulties with disgust. These different problems would not occur with a single system.

DEFICITS IN OBJECT PERCEPTION AND FACE PERCEPTION: VISUAL OBJECT AGNOSIA AND PROSOPAGNOSIA

Both the terms *agnosia* and *prosopagnosia* derive from Greek. Literally, *agnosia* means 'without knowledge'. Thus, visual object agnosia is 'without knowledge of visually perceived objects'. Prosopagnosia derives from *prosopon* (face) + *agnosia*, hence, 'without face knowledge'.

Agnosia results from brain damage. Visual agnosia relates to deficits in visual perception and visual recognition which cannot be attributed to visual problems, or issues with memory or language. Traditionally, two kinds of agnosia have been distinguished: *apperceptive agnosia* and *associative agnosia*. The former involves deficits in perceptual processing which lead to recognition problems, while with the latter, there is intact perceptual processing accompanied by dysfunctional recognition (see summary table).

	APPERCEPTIVE AGNOSIA	ASSOCIATIVE AGNOSIA
Perceptual Processing Deficit	*yes*	*no*
Recognition Deficit	*yes*	*yes*

In more detail, apperceptive agnosia involves an inability to create a well-structured representation of an object, which results in being unable to recognize objects. For example, one of the deficits exhibited by those with the disorder is an inability to copy line drawings of objects, which indicates (along with other evidence) that there is a problem in creating objects' representations. Given that, usually, objects which cannot be copied can be drawn from memory, knowledge about objects' appearances evidently remains intact. While object recognition cannot be achieved visually, if the object is picked up and held, touch information from the hands can be used to identify the object. Somewhat similarly, if the object is associated with a sound, (e.g., a bell), its auditory information can be used for recognition via hearing.

With associative agnosia, an object's form can be perceived accurately, but this cannot be linked to knowledge about the object held in memory, such as experiences of the object or its name. Consequently, the perceived object lacks an associated meaning. Typically, someone with associative agnosia can both copy and draw an object but cannot provide information about what the object is for, how it should be used, the object category from which it was drawn, or its name. Again, though, object identification may occur via touch.

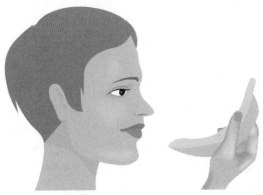

Apperceptive agnosia: *the object in the woman's hand cannot be recognized due to a perceptual processing deficit that prevents her from creating a well-structured representation of the banana. However, the object can be recognized using tactile information from her hand.*
Associative agnosia: *the banana's visual form can be perceived, but this cannot be linked to prior object concerning the object: for example, the viewed banana cannot be identified as 'fruit' or named. Tactile information can be used to recognize the object.*

However, although the apperceptive versus associative subdivisions make a useful distinction between agnosia types, evidence indicates that a two-type classification is too simplistic. Although the differences described appear clear cut, the distinction between apperceptive agnosia and associative agnosia are not actually so straightforward. Additionally, two subdivisions do not capture the different kinds of visual object agnosia that have been identified, examples of which are provided overleaf. Please note, however, that the deficits described are not complete: the information provided is intended to give the reader a very small idea of these different visual object agnosias.

Visual form agnosia and *integrative agnosia* are both apperceptive types of the disorder. With the former, a shape perception deficit is present such that even simple shapes cannot be copied, matched according to shape, or identified. The cause of this arises from the specific details of shapes failing to be grouped to form representations of surfaces and contours. In contrast, shape representations can be created in integrative agnosia because shapes can be copied and matched. However, the subsequent stage of grouping these representations into whole objects, or even into a whole detailed part of an object, cannot be achieved. This means that object recognition cannot proceed using information about the whole object and so, instead, an object's overall identity is assessed according to its various parts. Knowledge of objects is clearly unaffected, since they can be both drawn and described from memory.

Impaired access to structural knowledge is an example of associative visual object agnosia. It involves an intact ability to create perceptual representations of shapes, since even difficult objects can be copied and matched. However, as the objects successfully copied and matched cannot be identified, there is a problem in accessing structural representations of objects previously stored in memory.

Another kind of associative agnosia relates to *accessing semantic knowledge* about an object. In other words, accessing knowledge related to an object's meaning. The ability to copy and match objects indicates perceptual representations can be created, and, since objects can be drawn from memory, structural representations of objects held within memory can be accessed. However, problems arise with producing information which indicates knowledge about the object's meaning, such as being unable to identify a hammer as a hammer.

Turning now to prosopagnosia, those with this disorder fail to recognize known faces as familiar. This includes the faces of family members, friends and celebrities, as well as the faces of new people who are encountered. Failure to recognize these people is not the product of impaired visual ability or another psychological problem and it has consequences which go beyond face recognition, too.

Inability to recognize a familiar face also means that other information held concerning the person to whom the face belongs cannot be accessed, such as their occupation, interests, where they live, or their name. For example, with the earlier photograph of Marilyn Monroe (and assuming that she is sufficiently well known to the person with prosopagnosia), failure to recognize her face as familiar means that she cannot be identified as a female actor or named as *Marilyn Monroe*.

Since it is impossible for those with prosopagnosia to access person recognition information or names from a familiar face, they resort to using other information as a means of recognition. This might involve utilizing distinctive facial features such as a goatee beard or a large broken nose, and/or distinctive facial accessories, including spectacles, a nose ring, or earrings. Person recognition may also occur from the person's voice, or other clues such as hairstyle, a particular item of clothing, or the way in which the person walks.

There are two forms of prosopagnosia: *acquired* and *developmental*. With acquired prosopagnosia, there are intact face recognition abilities until brain damage leads to the disorder. Subsequently, a person is usually aware that their face recognition ability is no longer what it was. For example, one man who suffered brain damage after a motorcycle accident reported that, thereafter, faces were no longer the same. He couldn't tell who people were and had to wait for people to speak, otherwise he couldn't identify them. One day, he had gone to a party and met another man in the corridor; when he shifted to move out of the way so did the other man. After this had happened a few times, it grew annoying. Determined to move forward, he then discovered that the annoying man was actually a mirror reflection of himself. The individual who had become prosopagnosic could not recognize his own face, even though he saw it every day in the mirror when he shaved, combed his hair and checked his appearance. He knew that this error would never have arisen prior to the brain damage that produced his acquired prosopagnosia.

Developmental prosopagnosia is different in that brain damage isn't present, nor is there a point in time where there is a notable shift in face recognition ability: the deficit has always been present. Of the two kinds, acquired prosopagnosia has the longer investigative history, and consequently, its three subdivisions are considered below.

Prosopagnosia.

In apperceptive prosopagnosia, an accurate perceptual representation of a face's structure cannot be created. This means that there is insufficient structural information for face recognition to occur, nor is it possible to perceive the difference between different faces. Problems exist too in recognizing facial expressions. (In terms of Bruce and Young's model, there is a difficulty at the level of structural encoding.)

With associative prosopagnosia, face perception remains largely intact. However, there is a disconnection between the perceptual representation of a face and stored structural information concerning the face that is held in memory. Consequently, faces can be discriminated but they are not recognized as familiar, which, in turn, means identity information about the face cannot be accessed either. (Following the Bruce and Young model, although structural encoding of faces takes place, the face recognition units fail to be activated.)

Finally, amnestic prosopagnosia is identical to associative prosopagnosia except, instead of there being a disconnection to stored facial representations in memory, facial memories are lost.

Key Points

- Light travels through the different parts of the eye and electrochemical changes occur in nerve cells to produce a visual sensation. Visual perception involves applying meaning to visual sensation.
- Colour perception has been explained using the Trichromatic Theory and Opponent Process Theory.
- Perception involves detecting depth and employing shape and size constancy.
- Gestalt psychologists argued that we 'group' information and proposed different laws of perceptual grouping.
- Template Theory and Feature Theory were early explanations of pattern detection.
- Object recognition has been explained in the work of David Marr, Keith Nishihara, (primal sketch, 2½-D sketch, 3-D model representation) and Irving Biederman's Recognition by Components Theory.
- Face recognition is explained in Bruce and Young's model.
- Visual object agnosia involves deficits in the visual perception and recognition of objects and it can take different forms.
- Developmental and acquired prosopagnosia involve deficits in face processing. Acquired prosopagnosia has different forms.

Chapter 3

Attention

Your senses constantly provide you with incoming information. It is impossible to focus upon everything, so instead you select certain environmental aspects for processing and ignore others: this is *attention*. Or, to be more precise, this is what Marvin M. Chung and colleagues refer to as *external attention*. *Internal attention* they conceive as being present when you deal with internal information. It is involved when you select from the huge quantity of information held in your memory; decide what to do; pursue the relevant actions and achieve all of this effectively, over the required length of time. Attention is therefore hugely important in our daily activities.

Attention is characterized in other ways. When focus is devoted to a particular aspect of the environment, this is called *selective* or *focused attention*; when focus is given to two or more sets of information at the same time, this is *divided attention*, also known as *multitasking*. Psychologists also distinguish between *top-down* and *bottom-up* attention. Top-down attention is goal-driven: mental activity is concentrated upon a particular stimulus, such as focusing on the discovery of one item of clothing among others in your wardrobe; or focusing on this book while ignoring people and other objects about you. With bottom-up attention, something in the environment and external to us attracts attention, such as your desk light suddenly going off, a fire alarm sounding, or a person suddenly interrupting your reading.

In the box below, a situation is described with which you may be familiar. If you do not travel by train, substituting some other activity such as going to a busy shop, sports event, concert, or social event will allow you to gain an idea of the frequency with which attention is used (in **bold**).

You and your friend Lachie have arrived at a busy mainline station to catch a train. Lachie has gone to buy a coffee and you are **looking for his face among the other passengers** because he's now been away for a while. You **notice your mobile phone beeping** and you **read the text message** that's come through. When you look up, **you see Lachie is making his way toward you**, through the crowd. When he arrives, the two of you start **chatting** – another conversation added to those going on about you.

Since it is important that you know the platform from which your train will depart, you **check the departure boards**. Now, **whilst continuing your conversation, you're also keeping an eye on the relevant board** so that you will know when the platform opens.

When the time comes to board the train, you **take out your tickets and the two of you go to the automated gates, pass your tickets through the machine and walk through to the platforms**. As you have used the station before, **you know exactly where the relevant platform is and walk there directly**, Lachie hurrying along beside you.

FOCUSED/SELECTIVE AUDITORY ATTENTION

Let's begin with your ability to have a conversation with Lachie despite there being other conversations going on around you and other station-related noises being heard too. In other words, your ability to selectively attend to Lachie despite the presence of multiple competing sounds.

As you are listening to Lachie, unwanted sounds are filtered out and Lachie's voice is deliberately selected for focus using top-down processes. However, what is being attended in Lachie's speech that allows you to focus specifically on what he is saying, given the speech sounds in all the other conversations? This problem was investigated in 1953 by Colin Cherry, when he explored what he called the 'cocktail party problem'.

Cherry used two innovative techniques – *dichotic listening* and *shadowing*. The former involves simultaneously presenting research participants with two different auditory messages, one to the left ear and one to the right ear. Attention is focused on one of the messages – the designated target message. Shadowing repeats the format of dichotic listening but is different in that the attended message has to be repeated aloud verbatim while it is being presented. This ensures that all target messages receive consistent attention.

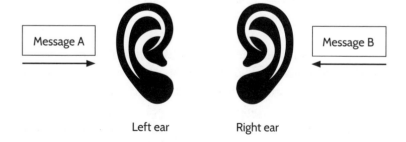

Message A → Left ear   Right ear ← Message B

Dichotic Listening: *Two different messages are simultaneously presented to the ears, one to the left ear and one to the right ear. Attention must be focused on the target message.*

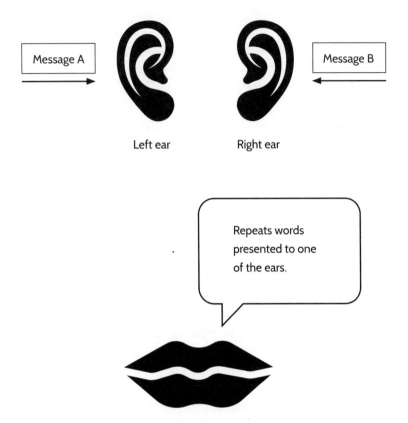

Shadowing: *Two different messages are simultaneously presented to the ears, one to the left ear and one to the right ear. The participant repeats aloud and verbatim what is presented to one of the ears.*

Cherry found that when it was possible to rely on voices' different physical attributes (such as location, speaker's sex, or intensity of the voice), then it was possible to tell the messages apart. However, if the same speaker spoke both messages, and thus differences between the messages had to be detected relying upon meaning alone, distinguishing between the two became very difficult. Little was gleaned from the unattended message; it only gained attention if there was a change in its physical characteristics, such as loudness, or if the person's name was mentioned.

Based on these results, you can attend to your conversation with Lachie based on the direction of his voice and other physical characteristics associated with his voice. More recent research, however, has revealed that you would make use of other information than that mentioned so far. For instance, we are familiar with friends' voices – even without seeing evidence of who is speaking, a voice alone can be sufficient to identify someone – and this familiarity can help us work out what is being said among all the other conversations.

Additionally, while chatting, people usually look at each other and take turns in contributing to the conversation which would add to your paying attention to what Lachie was saying. As the previous chapter's discussion of Bruce and Young's model of face processing revealed, visual facial information is used for speech analysis. Looking at Lachie's face could have assisted you with focusing attention on what he said. During his turns in the conversation, certain sound qualities would be associated with Lachie's voice, but they would disappear during your turns and when you were both silent. In more technical terms, *temporally coherent sound modulations* would be present as Lachie spoke. This means that, while speaking, changes, such as in loudness and pitch, bind sounds together and are present when Lachie is speaking but absent when he is silent. These temporally coherent sound modulations help Lachie's speech to be separated from other voices.

THEORIES OF ATTENTION

Different theories of attention have been proposed by psychologists. An early, historically important, information-processing theory was forwarded by Donald Broadbent in 1958. Broadbent's research on selective attention stemmed from practical problems faced by air traffic controllers as aviation increased during the Second World War. They were frequently required to attend to one message from among multiple other messages being sent by pilots at the same time.

From his dichotic listening and shadowing experiments, Broadbent determined that when we are presented with more than one auditory input, we cannot attend to everything at once. In his *filter theory*, Broadbent proposed that, initially, all incoming auditory information is briefly held in a *sensory buffer*. Subsequent to the sensory buffer, there is a *selective filter*, which prevents too much information gaining access to short-term memory and thereby overburdening its limited capacity. The selective filter allows attended information through, based on its physical attributes, but it does not allow unattended information to pass through. The auditory input remaining in the sensory buffer is lost from processing unless it is attended very quickly.

Applying this to your conversation with Lachie, you are able to attend to what he is saying despite the other conversations

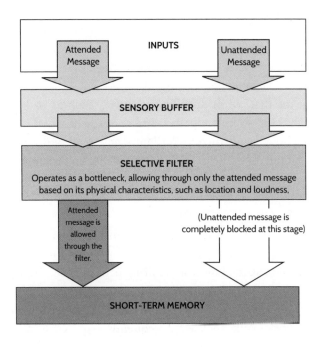

The Filter Theory of Attention.

Donald Broadbent.

because the selective filter operates like a bottleneck. That is, it prevents too much information getting through the system and, in our scenario, allows through Lachie's voice from among all the other conversations. Or, to put this another way, very early on, Lachie's voice is selected for attention, and this focused attention to his voice occurs in a bottom-up way.

Within the history of cognitive psychology, Broadbent's theory is significant because its information-processing approach has been adopted many times and with different cognitive topics. It also explained how the cocktail party problem is dealt with and provided a detailed account of attention that could be subjected to scrutiny. This led to further investigations, by other researchers, which revealed that unattended information is not filtered out in the way Broadbent's theory proposed. For example, meaningful content, in a supposedly unattended message, can attract attention. This is problematic because, if supposedly unattended information has been processed for meaning, then this is inconsistent with the idea of an early filter which allows through only attended information based upon its physical characteristics. Attention to meaning is not the product of bottom-up processing; instead, it involves top-down mental activity.

Anne Treisman argued that if the meaning of a supposedly unattended message receives attention, some of that message's content must have 'leaked' through the filter and undergone further processing. Consequently, she proposed that the supposedly unattended message isn't lost but *attenuated*, that is, weakened or diminished. What remains within the attenuated message may then undergo top-down processing.

As with Broadbent's account of focused attention, Treisman's *Attenuation Theory* begins with auditory input first being held within a *sensory buffer*. Again, due to the limited capacity of short-term memory, messages are analysed according to their physical characteristics and are then dealt with by the *attenuator*. The attenuator acts like a filter that weakens all auditory messages

Anne Treisman alongside US president, Barack Obama.

except for those which are attended. In this way, unattended messages, though diminished by the attenuator, are nevertheless available for later processing for meaning. However, unattended stimuli will only receive later processing if there is sufficient capacity available for this.

Compared with Broadbent's account, Treisman's theory allows more than one location for a bottleneck in processing. As with Broadbent, a bottleneck can occur early when selecting a message according to its physical characteristics, but one can also occur later, when processing for meaning.

A third theory forwarded by J.A. Deutsch and D. Deutsch was later extended by Donald Norman. This model of attention contends that all input is fully analysed and then filtering occurs nearer to the 'response' part of the processing system. By the time the filter is reached, some information will have been designated as the most relevant for making a response and it is this message that enters conscious awareness, within short-term memory. As with Broadbent's conceptualization, there is a filter which produces selective attention, but, instead of selective attention occurring early, it takes place late and this is where the bottleneck arises.

Which of the last two theories is likely to be correct? It is fair to say that some experts have doubted that selective attention takes place as late as contended by Deutsch, Deutsch and Norman. Treisman's theory has been criticized – along with all filter/bottleneck theories – for being too inflexible. It is perhaps, therefore, unsurprising that more flexible models of attention have been put forward that allow for adaptability in the point at which selective attention takes place.

William Johnston and Steven Heinz's *Multimode Theory* is an example of a more flexible model of selective attention. It maintains that selective attention can occur at different stages of processing. Selection can occur early based on physical information, such as the sex of a voice, but if selection is based upon meaning, then it occurs later.

FOCUSED VISUAL ATTENTION

In our station scenario, the place is busy. There are lots of people around; all the usual paraphernalia found at a mainline station are there such as shops, seating, left luggage facilities, information boards and information desks to help you travel. There's lots to see, but at any one time only part of the visual scene will be selected for attention. How is this accomplished?

Research from Michael Posner and colleagues led to the *Spotlight Theory* of focused visual attention. When the eyes fixate on something this involves focused attention which the viewer has controlled. However, attention can also shift to a different part of space, *without moving the eyes*, if cued to do so by an external stimulus. This is *covert attention*. Of course, whatever is the subject of covert attention may go on to be fixated by the eyes so that it may be seen more clearly.

Using the spotlight analogy, focused visual attention operates as if there is a mental spotlight shining down on what is being attended. Its beam lights up whatever is being given attention so that it receives priority processing. When the beam moves from one location to another (remember, this is without physical eye movement), attention is shifted to this part of the visual field.

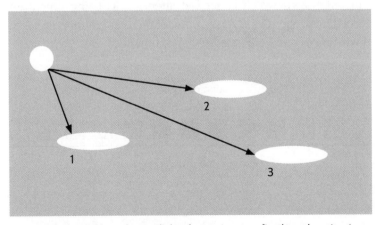

A representation of how the spotlight of attention may first be at location 1, then shift to location 2 and then to location 3.

The spotlight model was later extended by Charles W. Eriksen and James D. St. James in their *zoom lens* approach. As its name implies, this model operates akin to a camera's zoom lens. That is, the size of the area of attentional focus, or spotlight, can be adjusted to be broad or narrow.

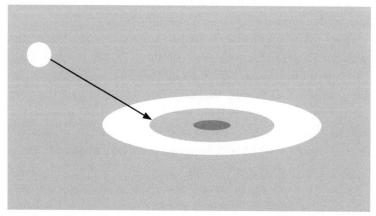

A representation of the zoom lens model. The original spotlight is in the middle and it can be made smaller (darker in the image) or larger (white).

A different kind of account was forwarded by David LaBerge and Vincent Brown which conceived attention as being organized according to a gradient. At the point of focus attention is greatest. As distance from here increases, attention decreases.

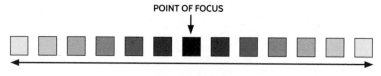

A representation of the gradient account. Attention is greatest at the point of focus – the black square in the middle. As distance from here increases, attention decreases as represented by the increasingly lighter squares.

All of the models discussed thus far have something in common: attention cannot be split or divided across different locations. Evidence indicates, though, that it is possible – at least under certain circumstances – to divide attention. This has led to *Split Attention* accounts, which propose that there can be multiple spotlights of attention, such that attention is split across more than one non-contiguous regions of space, with the areas in between being mostly ignored.

Fortunately, it is not essential to insist on choosing a single theory as the correct one for all circumstances. Instead, distribution of focused visual attention may well depend on what the viewer wants or needs to accomplish in their current circumstances. Indeed, research shows that sometimes the focus of visual attention is not an area of space at all, but an object or objects, or a particular feature. For example, if looking for a book on your shelf, it may be more efficient to look for the 'really big book', when this feature readily distinguishes one item from a number of very similar others.

Looking for the 'really big book' is an example of *visual search*, and in this instance size is sufficient to locate the object concerned. However, suppose the task is much more complex than this. Let us suppose that you are trying to locate a particular psychology textbook from the substantial number that are stored on your shelves. Unfortunately, the fixed height of the shelves combined with the publications coming in an assortment of sizes means that the books have not all been neatly arranged by topic. It is unlikely that you will read through the titles on every book spine to locate the desired text. Instead, you might recall that the book is not particularly tall and so does not have a long spine. Those books that have a long spine can be ignored. However, a number of books are the appropriate height and so another, different feature must be sought instead, such as spine width. If several books are the right height and width then another feature must be sought like colour, and so on, until the visual search has sufficiently narrowed down your options.

Books on shelves. A visual search of the shelves for a particular text can proceed by giving visual attention to the feature or features which will identify the desired text most efficiently. These features could include spine height, width and colour.

VISUAL SEARCH THEORIES

Anne Treisman's *Feature Integration Theory* is a two-stage model of visual search which contends that there is a difference in the cognitive processing that takes place before, versus after, focused visual attention. Historically, this is a very significant model because of the long influence it has had upon psychologists' approaches to the topic of attention. Along with Garry Gelade, Treisman conducted a number of different visual search experiments which involved participants searching for a target item among distractor items. The distractors varied in number, so there were more or fewer items to search through and they also varied according to their similarity or dissimilarity to the target.

In one study, this framework was applied to an experiment which reflected what is involved when we search for a single feature versus searching for more than one feature. When seeking the single feature, participants had to find either a letter S, or a blue letter T, or a blue letter X among different numbers of distractor items. These comprised the letter T in brown ink and the letter X in green ink, in as near equal numbers as possible (see box overleaf). With this task, it is possible to find the target by quite different shape (S versus T, X), or by colour (blue versus brown/green). When participants were required to search for more than one feature, their target was a green T among distractor items consisting of brown Ts and green Xs. Now, the target could only be found when there was a conjunction of colour and shape.

The researchers timed how long it took to detect the target. When a conjunction of colour and shape had to be found (T_{green}), locating the target took longer, the greater the number of items that had to be searched through. However, when searching could take place according to one feature alone, (S or T_{blue} or X_{blue}), the number of items to be searched through had very little effect on the time taken to detect the target. From this it was concluded that combining features necessitates focused visual attention, whereas this was not required when searching for a single feature. This led to Feature Integration Theory's two stages. Initially, there

	TARGET	DISTRACTORS
Single feature	*one of*	
	S	T_{brown}
	T_{blue}	X_{green}
	X_{blue}	
	Search can be by shape or colour	
More than one feature	T_{green}	T_{brown}
		X_{green}
	Search involves a conjunction of shape and colour	

is the *preattentive, parallel processing* stage. During this phase, individual features such as size, colour, shape or line orientation are processed quickly, without attention, all at the same time. At stage two, individual features are bound together using slower, *serial processing*. This means that one by one, features are bound together to produce the representation of an object so that T_{green} or any other object can be recognized. Focused attention to the location of an object is the means by which binding takes place.

Subsequently, working with Sharon Sato, Treisman refined her Feature Integration Theory. Binding two sets of information does not always necessitate a serial search of every item to locate a target. For example, if your target was a T_{blue} among distractors consisting of X_{green}, X_{blue}, T_{green}, you could happily ignore X_{green} because it has neither of the features of the target. Hence, it was proposed visual search is affected by how similar distractor items are to the target. If it is possible to eliminate an element from a search, the search will be faster.

Another account of visual search comes from Jeremy Wolfe and colleagues, who argued that preattentive feature processing

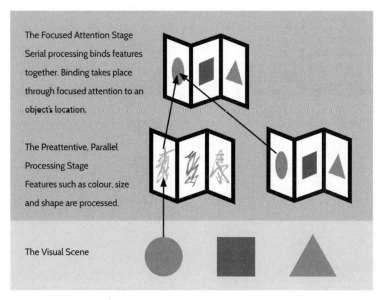

The Focused Attention Stage Serial processing binds features together. Binding takes place through focused attention to an object's location.

The Preattentive, Parallel Processing Stage Features such as colour, size and shape are processed.

The Visual Scene

Feature Integration Theory.

guides later, serial attention. In the *Guided Search 2.0* model, visual search begins with feature information being extracted. However, what is then designated for attention is a location selected from a map of prospective attentional locations.

Each prospective attentional location on the map has a different level of activity according to what is being sought in the visual search. Information held within memory concerning the target is important, such as whether we remember the target as being 'blue' (*top-down processing*). Furthermore, if, let's say, the search is for something 'big' and 'blue', these characteristics will be salient features in whatever we are visually searching for (*bottom-up processing*). Together, these sources contribute to the activity of locations on the map. In this way, if the target was T_{blue}, then X_{green} will have insufficient activation for attention because it does not possess the target's relevant features. X_{blue} and T_{green}, on the other hand, possess relevant features and therefore would have activation on the map, but as they are distractors the location would be suppressed.

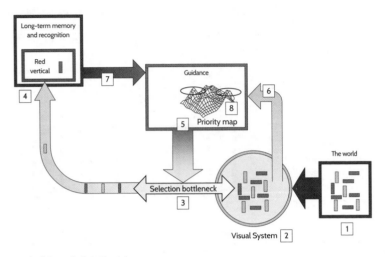

Guided Search 2.0 Model.

Later, Wolfe produced his *Guided Search 6.0* model. This retained the features of its predecessor and increased the sophistication of the account of guided search. What follows affords a simplified and incomplete discussion of 6.0's modifications but still provides extra details to how visual search takes place according to the 6.0 model.

In addition to top-down and bottom-up processing providing guidance as to what should be attended, version 6.0 has three other forms of guidance. One of these involves the *history* of where attention has been previously. Another form comes from the *value* assigned to features: for instance, in relation to the example used above, if the feature 'blue' is rewarded, whereas 'green' is punished, this assigns a value to the features and more attention will be given to rewarded features. The third additional form of guidance relates to the structure and meaning of *scenes*. When we conduct a visual search in daily life, the scene itself provides guidance: if you are looking for your pet dog, you would look at places such as the path or grass but you wouldn't look at the branches of trees or in the sky. Likewise, if you are seeking your friend's car you won't look at those places a car could not be; similarly, in the station, if you are searching for the departure boards, you wouldn't be looking at those places where such information would not be positioned.

A pet owner visually searching for her dog. Wolfe's Guided Search 6.0 model proposes that the structure and meaning of scenes help guide visual search. The owner searches for her dog in places that it is likely to be rather than in places it cannot be.

Guided Search 6.0 also distinguishes the roles of long-term memory and short-term, visual working memory in visual search. Imagine you are looking for a 30 cm (12 in) ruler. Two of visual working memory's roles are: holding a visual representation of the object that has been selected for attention; and holding the template which guides you to relevant attributes of what you are seeking, such as 'long' and 'thin'. Activated long-term memory holds a different kind of template concerning information applicable to looking for the ruler. This template is matched against working memory's representation of the object that has been selected for attention, to decide if that object is the ruler you were looking for.

The final visual search model to be considered is the very different *Texture Tiling Model* proposed by Ruth Rosenholtz and colleagues. The model's name relates to how visual input is organized and it contends that if viewing conditions are normal, selective attention is not required either for perception or to bind individual features together. Instead, it is argued that during the early stages of visual processing there is a considerable loss of information, particularly in the periphery of vision. Put very simply, if the perceptual representation of what is in the visual field contains sufficient peripheral information to allow attention to be directed to the target, then conducting a visual search will be easy. However, if the information is too little to permit attention to be directed to the target, visual search will be difficult.

In evaluating the models discussed, Treisman's original Feature Integration Theory did not stand the test of time; indeed, Treisman herself made changes to its ideas. Beyond this, it remains to be seen what will be the best account of attention and visual search.

DIVIDED ATTENTION

Divided attention, or multitasking, involves trying to complete two or more tasks concurrently. An example of this occurred in the previous station scenario when you held a conversation

Multitasking.

with Lachie while keeping an eye on the destination boards. You probably multitask in this way so often that you scarcely notice that it is happening. How often do you make a meal while listening to a podcast, music, or holding a conversation? It's also not uncommon to see people reading or sending messages on their mobile phones as they walk along the street. Parents have been known to worry if their offspring appear to be studying or completing assignments to the accompaniment of music, television, or other media.

Anecdotal evidence may give us the impression that multitasking can be productive and effective. A skilled, non-professional cook, highly familiar with a frequently prepared recipe, may pursue food preparation efficaciously while following an exciting radio drama. Similarly, proficient knitters can progress a garment and watch television at the same time. Experienced drivers chat to passengers while negotiating the road. However, is it really possible to multitask successfully?

Using a mobile phone while driving increases the chance of having a crash.

David Sanbonmatsu and colleagues found evidence that individuals' perceived ability to multitask does not reflect their actual ability to do so. Other research indicates that, generally speaking, performance decreases when we try to complete two tasks simultaneously and that we will perform more effectively by dealing with one task at a time.

Important research in this regard relates to mobile phone usage. In the UK, it is illegal to hold and use a phone while driving, though it may be operated with appropriate 'hands-free' access. Many other countries have similar regulations in place. This is not simply the result of hands being needed for the steering wheel, manually changing gear or adjusting instruments such as windscreen wipers: divided attention has the potential for serious consequences. Research reveals that using a phone notably increases the chances of having a crash. For example, it can: reduce response times (including those to brake lights); lead to speeding and failure to maintain an appropriate distance from other vehicles, and cause eye glances that would detect hazards to be reduced.

Of course, given that anecdotal observations show that drivers can chat with a passenger and drive at the same time, it is tempting to think such conversations may not be especially different in nature from those held on a mobile phone. Experts, however, disagree with this position. David L. Strayer and colleagues' research has highlighted a number of important differences between the two. They found that if road conditions were difficult, there would be a pause with passenger conversations until driving circumstances improved, but this did not occur with mobile phone conversations. Furthermore, with a passenger, there were more mentions of traffic within the conversation than with the person on the other end of the mobile phone. Passengers also assisted the driver by helping to navigate and identifying hazards. Consequently, it is possible to conclude that the division of attentional resources does not operate in the same way with passenger versus mobile phone conversations.

It is also tempting to think that 'practice always makes perfect' and, therefore, all that is needed to improve dividing attention between driving and talking on a mobile is practice. Using a driving simulator, Strayer and colleagues found that this was not the case. Their results showed that although practice helped reduce collisions when the scenario and events within it did not change over four days of practice, there were still more crashes when using a mobile than when not doing so. Moreover, when a new set of driving circumstances had to be undertaken, the effects of practice were lost. Since driving circumstances are rarely, if ever, absolutely identical and mobile phone conversations are not identical either, practising driving whilst holding a mobile phone conversation will not lead to an improved ability to divide attention between the two tasks.

How, then, does divided attention lead to crashes?

Strayer and different colleagues forwarded the following explanation. Mental resources are required for driving and they are also required for holding a conversation on a mobile phone: that is, there is a cognitive workload for each. When driving without holding a conversation, mental resources are concentrated on driving and this is the only workload. However, when conversing on a mobile phone, this second task diverts attention from driving (it is a cognitive distraction). As the mental resources, or cognitive workload, increase as a result of the conversation, fewer mental resources are available for driving, due to attentional resources being limited. Attempting to do two things at once reduces success at driving appropriately and thus crashes are more likely to occur.

Nevertheless, daily life shows us that we do appear to multitask successfully sometimes. The anecdotal evidence of the television-watching knitter plus the skilled amateur cook who is listening to the radio drama surely show this? According to Michael Eysenck and Mark Keane, an ability to do two things at once depends upon task similarity and practice. The kind of practice referred to here is the sort which allows for task repetition.

Task similarity refers to how alike two tasks are and whether we are required to respond to them in the same way or not. For example, let's suppose our cook is preparing a recipe which involves watching carefully for the point when ingredients reach a particular consistency. As this is a visual task, while listening to a drama is an auditory one, research evidence indicates that performing the tasks simultaneously can be achieved because they do not impose similar demands. However, if the individual was listening to the drama and then also had to attend to another person in the room who is speaking, this would now involve two auditory inputs. These inputs, being too similar, would interfere with each other and, thus, following both equally successfully would be hard.

A comparable principle applies in relation to what is required of us in order to complete two tasks at the same time. Research results reveal that if we are required to perform similar actions, then this will make multitasking harder than if the actions are not alike.

These anecdotal examples above include instances of where practice permits multitasking. Skilled cooks not only repeat – and therefore practise – recipes but also do likewise with assorted food preparation techniques. Accomplished knitters repeat and become practised at types of stitch; they also become practised at repeatedly producing line after line of a repeating pattern. Stiches can be produced without having to look at the needles, wool and stitch-making all the time. Experimental evidence also confirms the effects of practice on divided attention.

A well-known study was conducted by Elizabeth Spelke and colleagues using a *dual task* procedure. They had two undergraduate students read short stories – which had to be comprehended – while at the same time writing down dictated words. Initially, the students found what they were required to do extremely difficult. Yet, with practice consisting of five one-hour sessions per week, over 17 weeks, their ability to dual-task increased. They became able to read for comprehension at normal speed as well as being able to write words, identify

Elizabeth Spelke.

relations between dictated words and categorize words according to meaning. Spelke *et al.* concluded that attention is based on acquiring skills specific to what is demanded by the situation.

A question which has received considerable attention concerns how multitasking proceeds. If there are two tasks to attend, it is possible the cognitive processes required operate one at a time, or in series. On the other hand, they could operate at the same time, or in parallel. Reviewing the evidence, Rico Fischer and Franziska Plessow highlighted that these means of processing are not mutually exclusive and shifts between them depend on the conditions under which multitasking takes place. Other researchers have found evidence for individual styles of multitasking. For example, Jessika Reissland and Dietrich Manzey reported that some people prefer to work serially, while others prefer to interleave tasks with some overlapping of one task with the other.

AUTOMATIC PROCESSING VERSUS CONTROLLED PROCESSING

The implication with our television-watching knitter is that the person has become so adept at knitting that little conscious attention is required: knitting has become automated. In contrast, controlled processing necessitates conscious attention to the task at hand, such as when someone is learning to knit, or a more experienced knitter is dealing with a tricky part of a pattern. Riding a bike also demonstrates the difference between automatic and controlled processes. A proficient rider takes to the saddle and sets off; attention does not have to be devoted to the mechanics of riding a bike, only to the road conditions and whatever may be observed safely while cycling. A novice rider, on the other hand, must give attention to the act of bike-riding. It is essential to ensure the rider doesn't fall over; this requires endeavouring to balance and trying to pedal sufficiently fast to assist with this. Speed has its own risks, so going fast enough – but not too fast – needs attention too. The features of automatic and controlled processing are summarized in the table overleaf.

THE FEATURES OF AUTOMATIC PROCESSING VERSUS CONTROLLED PROCESSING	
AUTOMATIC PROCESSING	CONTROLLED PROCESSING
Attention not required	Attention required
Fast	Slow
Effortless	Effortful
Unavailable to conscious awareness	Conscious effort required
Fairly error free	Prone to error
Can be involuntary or unavoidable	Voluntary or avoidable
Can be accomplished alongside other cognitive processes	Interferes with other cognitive processes

That processing can be automatic or controlled was first established by Richard Shiffrin and Walter Schneider based on a series of memory experiments. These involved participants being presented with a row of consonants, or numbers, which had to be remembered. At test, participants quickly determined if any one of the items had been in the memory set. However, sometimes consistent mapping and at other times varied mapping were used between the memory task and test stimuli.

With consistent mapping, if the memory set consisted of consonants, the test set contained numbers, or a consonant amid numbers. In this way, if a consonant appeared in the test set, it had to have been in the memory set. Likewise, if the memory set comprised numbers, its test set contained consonants, or a number among consonants. Now, if a number appeared at test, it had to have been in the memory set. Varied mapping involved consonants and numbers in both memory and test sets. Now, it was harder to discern whether a memory set item was present or not.

Decision times were faster with consistent mapping than with varied mapping. This led Shiffrin and Schneider to conclude that the former was completed using automatic processing as a result of the years and years of repeated practice that the participants had of differentiating consonants versus numbers. Indeed, the researchers also experimentally confirmed that practice improves the ability to complete a consistent mapping task, confirming that automatic processing can proceed from practice. Yet, once established, automatic processing can be problematic because it continues to occur despite a change in circumstances for which it is no longer appropriate. With regard to varied mapping, this took longer because it necessitated controlled processing. Extensive attentional resources were required as items were processed one at a time, or in series.

Based on their studies, the researchers concluded that automatic processing does not require large amounts of attentional capacity; is unaffected by attentional capacity limits; is fast; is unavailable to conscious awareness; and can be unavoidable. Controlled processing, on the other hand, needs high levels of attentional capacity; is affected by attentional capacity limits; and involves consciously directing attention.

Applied to daily life, automatic processing, though often advantageous, can lead to us doing the wrong thing. For example, suppose you always travel a certain route walking home from your friend's house. This practised and established routine regularly gets you where you want to be and route-finding doesn't require much attention. Today though, you want to post a letter which requires a diversion along a street you wouldn't normally take. You stride along and walk past the end of the street with the letter box, as you've automatically slotted into your normal route. Similarly, students who have learned that certain kinds of assessment questions require a particular type of response, may automatically begin responding in that way unless they realize that the current question is different and needs a different kind of approach. Clearly, in this instance, a more controlled approach, which assesses the best kind of method to take with the question, would be more effective.

Although Shiffrin and Schneider regarded automatic processes as developing from extensive practice, their view was that controlled processing and automatic processing are distinct. A process is *either* automatic *or* it is controlled. A difficulty with this position is that it is hard to find processes that can be neatly categorized as *either* one *or* the other. Furthermore, evidence indicates that automaticity develops gradually and continuously with practice, and, as this takes place, processing becomes faster with less need for attention.

An account of how the transition to automaticity occurs can be found in the work of Gordon Logan, who argued that automatic processing results from directly accessing information from memory.

When something is done for the first time, a number of steps have to be gone through, in which rules are applied to reach a solution to the problem at hand. Each time practice occurs though, a memory is created and stored, and, with repeated practice, there is an accumulation of information. Ultimately, this allows a single solution to a problem to be arrived at without going through any intermediary stages first. In other words, instead of there being several steps to solving the problem, there is now just one, drawn from what is stored in memory. The move from going through a number of steps accompanied by the application of rules, to drawing solely from memory, is the point at which automaticity is established. As only a single step is now required, an automatic response is fast, effortless and unavailable to conscious awareness.

All this can be seen in bicycle riding. In order to cycle, the novice has different rules to apply to ensure that they stay upright, such as what must be accomplished to retain balance and pedal at the appropriate speed. The expert having practised all of this many times knows how to do this based upon what is stored in memory. Another example can be found in learning a new language. In Scots Gaelic, the name Mary is *Mairi* and of course,

An expert cyclist riding a bike. Novice cyclists use controlled processing when riding a bike because they have to consider all the different elements that are necessary to be successful. In contrast, experts use automatic processing when cycling: they are so practised at what is required that they don't have to devote attention to every aspect of cycling.

has its own pronunciation. When a name is called out though, a different form is used – vocative rather than nominative – and *Mairi* becomes *a Mhairi*. When learning Gaelic as a second language, the rules have to be gone through in relation to applying the correct form of spelling and pronunciation. With practice though, the speaker will automatically select the correct form for calling out the name.

A DEFICIT IN VISUAL ATTENTION: UNILATERAL SPATIAL NEGLECT

Unilateral Spatial Neglect is the inability to pay attention to the contents of one half of space due to damage to the brain. It has an estimated prevalence in 25–30 per cent of people who have a stroke. Most of these people have damage to their right hemisphere, or right half of the brain.

Unilateral Spatial Neglect's presence is observable in daily life, such as when a person ignores food on one side of a plate, collides with objects on one side of their surroundings, fails to look at an individual who is located on one side of their visual field, or when they pay attention to only one side of their face and body. All of these behaviours are associated with the side opposite the brain injury. Consequently, with damage to the right hemisphere, it is the left side of a plate which is ignored; attention isn't given to the person who is in the left side of space, and objects are bumped into within the left side of the person's surroundings. Additionally, only the right side of the body is washed and attended to with regard to dressing appropriately. The left side of the face goes unwashed, unshaved or without make-up; hair on the left side of the head is not combed or brushed.

The examples above collectively incorporate the three regions of space affected by Unilateral Spatial Neglect. If personal space is affected (*personal neglect*), then there is an inability to give attention to one side of the face and body. Beyond personal space, neglect may occur within reaching distance (*peripersonal neglect*), or to the sector of space that falls outside reaching distance (*extrapersonal neglect*). Eating and drinking are activities that fall within reaching difference. When the left half of a plate of food has been ignored, or a drink in the left half of space has gone unattended, moving the items into the right half of space will lead to their being consumed. Extrapersonal neglect involves overlooking the presence of people or objects. Naturally, bumping into objects can cause injury; however, the potential for worse injury exists in those situations where the successful detection of visual information is vital to safety, such as being aware of approaching vehicles in order to cross roads unscathed. Although each of the three forms of neglect can occur independently, they appear more commonly in combination.

Two tests are frequently used to test for Unilateral Spatial Neglect: *line bisection* and *cancellation*. As its name suggests, line bisection requires that a mark is made at the centre of a horizontal line. However, with Unilateral Spatial Neglect arising from right hemisphere damage, what usually happens is that the mark is drawn to the right of the line's mid-point. Cancellation involves a sheet of paper printed with different items; some of these are designated as targets and the remainder are distractor items. The cancellation task requires that target items should be cancelled out, for example by putting a ring round the targets. Although the targets appear to the left and to the right, only those on the right are typically cancelled.

Drawing and copying tests can be employed too. These provide an assessment of how the ability to represent objects has been affected; for example, information to the left of an object may be omitted, or, instead, information which belongs on the left may be inserted on the right. A representation of what may happen with copying can be seen in the image of the flower overleaf – only information from the right is included. A common drawing task involves providing an empty clock face into which the numbers 1–12 must be inserted. A representation of cramming left side information into the right side can be seen in the clock face image.

Original for copying

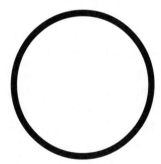

Original provided for drawing

Representations of how a person with Unilateral Spatial Neglect may copy an image of a flower and draw a clock face.

Key Points

- Attention can be characterized as external, internal, selective, divided, top-down and bottom-up.
- Selective auditory attention relies upon physical attributes such as location, speaker's sex, voice intensity, familiarity with the voice, conversational turn-taking and looking at each other during conversation.
- Filter theories of attention were proposed by Broadbent, Treisman and Deutsch and Deutsch; Johnston and Heinz proposed selective attention can occur at different stages of processing.
- Focused visual attention has been accounted for by Spotlight Theory, the Zoom Lens and Gradient approaches.
- Feature Integration Theory, Guided Search 2.0, Guided Search 6.0 and Texture Tiling are models of visual search.
- Divided attention involves completing two tasks concurrently; the perceived ability to multitask does not reflect the actual ability to do so. Limits on attentional resources affect multitasking as do task similarity and practice.
- Automatic and controlled processing are different; the former may develop through memory acquisition.
- Unilateral Spatial Neglect results from brain damage and is characterized by an inability to pay attention to the contents of one half of space.

Chapter 4

Memory

How many times do you think you have used your memory today? Once or twice? Repeatedly? Memory is used more often than we sometimes appreciate. This box may help you think about it.

Imagine that today, you make plans for a week on Saturday. You decide to go for a meal followed by a visit to the cinema. Your choices involve places with which you are very familiar.

At which points do you think you would use your memory for these activities? Below are a few instances of remembering:

1. Your plans for that Saturday.
2. The route to where you will eat and the route to the cinema.
3. How to drive a car, if you go by car; or, how to use a bus if travelling by public transport.
4. The procedure for ordering and paying for the food. This will be different according to whether you eat at a restaurant or opt for a fast-food outlet, for example.
5. Reading the menu and knowing what the items are, based on their names and descriptions.

6. The aroma rising from the brown liquid in your cup which identifies it as coffee.
7. Knowing that in the United Kingdom, you queue, if necessary, to buy your cinema ticket.
8. Following the plot of the film, its characters and what they say.
9. Identifying that the opening scene of the film is set in Egypt because there is a shot of the Sphinx and the pyramids.
10. Recalling that pyramids served as tombs.

In very simple terms, memory involves putting an item into memory (*encoding*); keeping it there (*storage*) and later accessing the stored item (*retrieval*). Retrieval can involve *recognition,* or identifying a stimulus as something which has been previously encountered, such as the experience of familiarity which arises when seeing the structures in the opening shot of the film. You recognize them as objects you have encountered before.

Recall involves a search through memory to retrieve information, such as the fact that the Sphinx is located in Egypt. Our efforts to recall information often only become apparent when there is some difficulty in retrieving information. In the case of the Sphinx, we may readily recall its location but perhaps spend longer attempting to recall that the specific animal represented in its body is a lion.

TYPES OF MEMORY

As mentioned in the Introduction, an early information-processing approach to memory was conceived by Richard C. Atkinson and Richard M. Shiffrin in their multi-store model. This proposed that memory consists of a *sensory store, short-term store* and *long term store.* The model is important because it was characteristic of other memory models then in existence and its contents helped generate considerable research. Greater research led to the original formulation of the model being questioned, but the three stores remain useful ways of thinking about the nature of memory.

The Sphinx and one of the pyramids at Giza.

The three types of memory proposed by Atkinson and Shiffrin in their multi-store model of memory.

Sensory memory involves the very brief storage of information detected by the senses. It is really more a feature of perception than memory. The sensory store allows us to glean information from sensory input by holding it long enough for it to be further evaluated. For example, if you stand in the dark, switch on a torch and swish it horizontally, diagonally and then horizontally again, you can 'write' the letter Z. However, by the time you are forming the last horizontal line, the torch is no longer providing visual stimulation for the first horizontal line, nor the diagonal line. Instead, the sensory store holds the visual information long enough for you to 'see' a Z.

The existence of visual sensory memory, or *iconic memory*, was demonstrated by George Sperling. He showed his participants stimuli comprising 12-letter arrays, arranged as three rows of four letters, for 1/20th of a second. For each stimulus, the task was to recall the array. Typically, four or five letters were remembered. However, participants often maintained that they had seen more items than they were able to report. Conceivably, more information had originally been held but faded away, or *decayed,* before it could be provided.

To test this, Sperling again presented the same kind of stimuli – three rows of four letters – but this time, at test, a tone sounded. A high tone signalled that the top row should be recalled; a medium tone the middle row, and a low tone that the bottom row should be recalled. Since participants had no idea which tone

A representation of George Sperling's iconic memory experiment, in which the sound of a tone (high, medium or low) signalled which line of a stimulus had to be recalled (top, middle, bottom). Here, the participant has heard a high tone and so recalls the top line of the stimulus.

would sound, the number of items reported for any given row could be multiplied by three to give an indication of how many letters in total were available for reporting, prior to their being lost by decay. In other words, it was possible to calculate the total number of letters held within visual, sensory memory based on one line alone. The results revealed that if the tone sounded just before or after the array was shown, the total number of letters available in sensory memory was 9 (3 being regularly reported from a given row x 3 rows = 9). Increasing the time between showing the array and playing the tone led to a drop in recall, which indicated that iconic memory decayed swiftly, within one half of a second.

With regard to the other senses, *echoic memory* is responsible for the brief storage of auditory information. Its duration lasts, on average, about four seconds, though evidence indicates there is some slight variation around this figure according to which half of the brain is retaining the information. Sensory stores also exist for touch, taste and smell; however, smell and taste are sufficiently closely related to make separate studies of these sensory stores difficult.

Whilst Atkinson and Shiffrin separated short-term memory (STM) and long-term memory (LTM), more recently this has been contested, and arguments have been forwarded that these kinds of memory are essentially the same. Others, though, do not adopt this position and regard short- and long-term memory as two different but related systems. For present purposes, having made the reader aware of this lack of uniformity, to preserve clarity within the discussion, STM and LTM will be treated separately, following the latter position.

'I was working with this information two days ago but I need to go through it again now. I have a terribly bad short-term memory!'

This quote is something you might hear from a student preparing for exams and is typical of how short-term memory is often understood outside the discipline of psychology. For a psychologist though, short-term memory does not relate to memories which are days, or even hours old. Instead, short-term memory is responsible for the temporary storage of information over several seconds and, ordinarily, for less than a minute. Long-term memory, on the other hand, refers to retaining information for longer periods – minutes, hours, days and even up to a lifetime.

In addition to being different in *duration*, STM and LTM are also different in terms of capacity. The wide variety and many memories that we hold over time demonstrate that the *capacity* of long-term memory is effectively unlimited. In contrast, STM's capacity is firmly limited.

The *span measures technique* has been a common way to assess the capacity of short-term memory. It involves presenting participants with a random series of items (either letters, or digits, or words) which, once the series has been completed, have to be repeated in the correct order. According to George Miller, the maximum that could be recalled was 5–9 chunks of information, or, as he put it in the title of his research report, *The Magical Number Seven, Plus or Minus Two*. Note that 7± 2 referred to *chunks* of information and not to individual items. What constitutes a chunk is determined by what is held in long-term memory: if you are familiar with the British motoring organization the RAC, for instance, the three letters become one chunk of information. Similarly, individual digits can constitute chunks if they create something familiar such as a date (1,9,4,5: 1945 the end of the Second World War), or a dialling code (0,1,7,3,8: 01738 the area code for Perth, Scotland).

As time progressed, however, research findings made changes to Miller's conclusions. STM capacity evidently could not be predicated on the number of chunks stored since chunk size affected memory: STM was poorer when chunks were longer. Furthermore, doubt was cast upon the figure of 7±2 reported by Miller when a number of studies reported a lower capacity, summarized as 4±1 by Nelson Cowan.

To address this discrepancy, Fabien Mathy and Jacob Feldman moved beyond the rather loose definition of chunk that can be seen in the examples given on the facing page, in which a chunk is a single unit of information consisting of individual items. Working from the perspective that information can be compressed, or represented in a more compact way, Mathy and Feldman defined a chunk as 'maximally compressed code'. In other words, chunks result from compressing data into the smallest number of possible sequences. What is meant by this can be seen by looking at the following list of numbers: 789642135. Do you notice anything about this sequence? The digits can be compressed as follows: in 789 there is an increase by a value of 1; in 642 there is a reduction by a value of 2; in 135 an increase occurs by a value of 2. A total of 9 digits may be reduced to 3 chunks.

From their experiments, it was concluded that the apparent discrepancy in STM capacity was the consequence of whether compression does or does not take place. In this way, neither figure of 7±2 nor 4±1 is wrong – their reference points are just different. Miller's figure reflects what occurs without compression while Cowan's figure captures what happens with compression. This is not to say, though, that one figure is not a better representation of short-term capacity than the other. Mathy and Feldman made clear that 4±1 best captures the size of STM because this figure represents the full amount of information that can be stored.

Another distinction that has been made between short- and long-term memory has been in terms of their preferred form of encoding with verbal material. Encoding refers to converting information from the senses into a form that can be used by memory. For example, if you were to hear a bell, its sound would be *acoustically encoded*. The scent of a rose results in *olfactory encoding*, the feel of its stem (smooth, thorny, soft, firm) in *haptic encoding* and its appearance is visually encoded. Taste, such as the flavour of strawberry ice cream or a cup of coffee, involves

George Miller.

The General Post Office headquarters.

gustatory encoding. Finally, *semantic encoding* comprises coding the meaning of information.

In the 1960s, the General Post Office – then responsible for Britain's state postal system and telecommunications service – asked Dr R. Conrad to investigate letter- and number-based codes. He visually presented multiple lists of 6-consonant sequences, which participants had to write down immediately after the stimulus presentation. However, some sequences consisted of consonants which sounded similar (e.g., T P V C B G), while the others sounded dissimilar (e.g., N M F X S K). With this short-term memory test, Conrad found that despite the visual presentation, more errors were made with acoustically similar consonants than with acoustically dissimilar ones. This led him to conclude that although the consonants could have been remembered in terms of how they looked, they were instead converted into an acoustic code.

A similar result was reported by Alan Baddeley who, in addition to investigating short-term memory, also tested long-term memory, using acoustically similar/dissimilar words and semantically similar/dissimilar words. Short-term memory for words was poorer when they sounded alike than when they did not, while meaning had little effect on participants' memories. Once again, despite a visual presentation, STM converted the words into acoustic code.

Baddeley's long-term memory results exhibited a different pattern, however. Here, most problems occurred with the words which possessed similar meanings. Thus, LTM favoured encoding semantically and the acoustic information from the words was not kept.

Since forgetting is a topic to be discussed in more detail over the following pages, for now it can simply be pointed out that STM and LTM differ in the way in which material is forgotten from their stores, and we can move on to focusing on neurological evidence. That is, evidence from people who have brain damage that has left one type of memory intact and the other one impaired. Perhaps

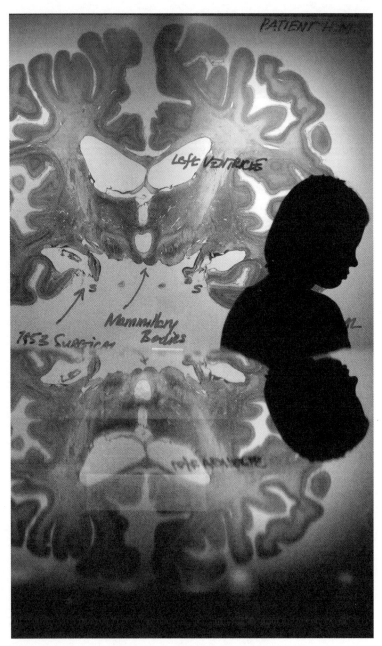

A slice of HM's brain. (Its reflection appears in the foreground).

the two most famous examples of this come from *case studies* of Patient KF and Henry Molaison. The term *case study* here refers to in-depth investigations of the two individuals' unimpaired and impaired memory performance.

Patient KF was tested by Tim Shallice and Elizabeth Warrington, who discovered that KF had unimpaired long-term recall and learning, alongside a deficit with STM, in that a very small digit span was observed. Investigations of Henry Molaison's memory by William Scoville and Brenda Milner had earlier revealed the opposite pattern: his short-term memory was effectively unimpaired while his long-term memories were affected, such as remembering that a conversation had taken place previously. As short-term memory and long-term memory may be impaired independently, this has been taken as evidence that they are different types of memory.

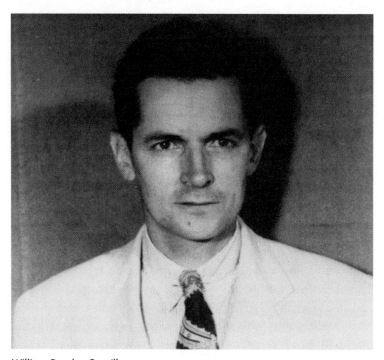

William Beecher Scoville.

The differences between STM and LTM discussed thus far may well have given the impression that short-term memory and long-term memory each ought to be considered as unitary. That is, that there is one, single STM and likewise, one single LTM. However, as we shall see later, this is not the case: there are different types of short- and long-term memories.

WORKING MEMORY

Task 1
Please read the following.

The boys waited and waited, then, all of a sudden, there it was! That unmistakable sound over the rooftops, the roar from the stadium...

Task 2
This task involves some simple mental arithmetic. It may be easier to read through a–c first before performing the calculation.

a) Add together 14 and 10.
b) Divide your answer by 2.
c) Now subtract 3.

Having completed the tasks above, you have just used your *working memory*. Working memory is the designation now used in place of the older terminology, short-term memory. Why is the newer name only being used here, now? Part of the reason is that the term short-term memory is still found within psychological literature and, of course, in older discussions of memory only that name was used. Additionally, given that much of the psychological thinking discussed above comes from the era when *short-term memory* was used, it was more appropriate to retain the original term.

Working memory is used in daily activities, during which, in all likelihood, we aren't especially aware of using memory. Task 1 is a relatively simple reading exercise, but for what you read to make sense you have to hold the information, briefly, in memory. This includes that it is the boys who are waiting, that they heard something that was unmistakable, where it came from and what it was. The same principle holds true of spoken language: if you are told: 'I'm going to visit the National Portrait Gallery at the end of April when I visit friends', you have to be able to recall who is going, where, when and with whom. If all this information cannot be held, then what is taking place is lost. Moreover, it must also be held in the appropriate order, to know who is doing what, where and when.

To perform the whole calculation of Task 2, you begin with determining the answer to $14 + 10$. Now, its product, 24, has to be held briefly in memory whilst the division by 2 occurs, yielding 12. The first result, 24, may now be discarded but 12 must be held in memory in order to subtract 3. The final answer, 9, is the one that you want, but memory was needed to get here. If this example appears to be too much like a school exercise, then when you want to know how much a couple of items are going to cost you in a shop, such as £3.60 + £2.47, summing their prices will involve working memory.

Here is another example of using working memory: suppose that you are looking for something that you know will be present but is not proving easy to locate. Perhaps you are seeking a specific product that you have purchased previously – and which you know should be on particular shelves in the supermarket – but a store reorganization has led to its being repositioned. You might look at the former, usual position of the item, then, being unsuccessful, go on to check another part of the shelves. If this is also unsuccessful, you will move on again to another section of relevant shelving. Note that having inspected one area, you do not rescan it, but move on to a different part of the shelves since it is unproductive to review the same area. You do not engage in fruitless reconsideration of those parts of the shelving just studied because working memory retains information concerning what you have just looked over.

Locating an item in a supermarket.

Problems with working memory can lead to difficulties in school, such as problems following teachers' instructions, paying attention, reading, spelling, and studying maths and science. Impairments in working memory have also been found in people with Alzheimer's Disease which can lead to difficulties with everyday tasks. Research has shown that those with Alzheimer's Disease experience difficulty if they are required to divide their attention.

A model of working memory was proposed by Alan Baddeley and Graham Hitch. In its original formulation it had three components: the *central executive, visuo-spatial sketchpad* and *phonological loop*; it was developed again by Baddeley when he added the *episodic buffer*.

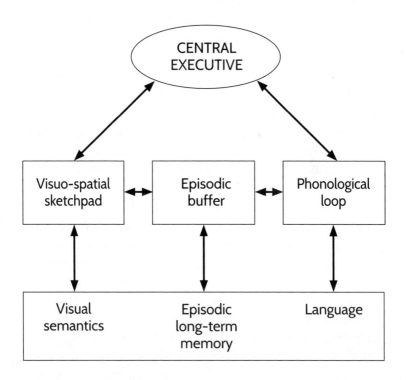

Working Memory Model.

The most important part of the model, the central executive, is also the component which is the least well understood, as a consequence of its being very difficult to investigate. Its importance lies in it having a supervisory role over working memory's other, subsidiary components.

Although the central executive cannot store information and has a limited capacity, it can process information from any of the senses. It also integrates information from the three other parts of the model, directs working memory, and operates along the lines of an attentional system. More specifically, the central executive is responsible for focusing attention, switching attention between different tasks, dividing attention appropriately between two sets of incoming information, and activating long-term memory to supply necessary stored information.

Relating this to everyday life, the central executive is involved in planning, problem solving and decision making, such as what should be done next and how it should be accomplished. If the selected approach is unsuccessful, the central executive is responsible for terminating this tactic. By choosing what requires attention and suppressing what should be ignored, the central executive also keeps you on task. However, due to its capacity restrictions, it cannot complete two very difficult tasks simultaneously, nor can it make multiple decisions concurrently.

As its name implies, the visuo-spatial sketchpad processes visual and spatial information. Visual information refers to what things look like, in terms of form and colour, such that the sketchpad captures the appearance of a scene and its associated objects. Spatial information concerns where things are positioned in space and movement information. Visuo-spatial information can be both stored, and mentally manipulated, within the sketchpad, but the sketchpad possesses limited storage capacity. Scanning for your item of shopping, in the example given above, would involve the visuo-spatial sketchpad, as would moving from place to place, or tracking a moving object. Sketching, tailoring, architectural drawing, watching television or a film in

Completing a jigsaw.

the cinema and completing a jigsaw are all examples of where the visuo-spatial sketchpad would be involved.

The phonological loop is sound-based and thus input to this component includes any environmental sound, including music and speech. It is sub-divided into the *phonological store* and *articulatory control process*, is responsible for storing word order and is involved in speech perception, speech production and reading. When words are heard, they automatically enter the phonological store which remembers speech sounds along with their order. This information is lost quickly, though, unless rehearsed (repeated) by the articulatory control process. The articulatory process also transforms text into phonological code when we read, thereby visual language can also access the phonological store. The phonological loop also holds information required to produce speech.

The characteristics of the episodic buffer are, unsurprisingly, that it is both episodic and a buffer. It is episodic in the sense that it holds information concerning events, episodes or scenes that have been experienced. It is a buffer because the temporary storage it affords allows the different parts of working memory to interact with each other using multidimensional code, in addition to which, a close interface is provided with perception and long-term memory.

To put this in more practical terms, if a friend walks past you and calls out a greeting, the visual and auditory information would arrive via different senses, in separate visual and auditory codes. However, your perception of the event would be that the visual and verbal elements occurred as a unified whole. Consequently, these separate visual and auditory representations must be brought together to form one, single experience and this happens at the episodic buffer. However, how much information can be chunked together is restricted by the episodic buffer's capacity, which is limited to about four episodes or chunks.

The working memory model proposed by Baddeley and Hitch has been extremely influential. Compared with Atkinson and Shiffrin's early view of short-term memory as simply one single store, the newer conceptualization was far more complex, with its multiple components and the manipulation of information. It explained why those with intact brains could cope with a visual short-term memory task, while simultaneously completing a verbal one, and it also accounted for neurological evidence in which brain damage led to only a partial deficit in short-term memory rather than a total loss. However, even those who support the idea of a multi-component working memory acknowledge that much is yet to be explained. Even with the addition of the episodic buffer the model remains over-simplified. Although other sensory input has not been ignored, the focus remains heavily on visual and verbal information and the model's individual components will inevitably be more complex, too.

ACQUIRING LONG-TERM MEMORIES

When we consciously or intentionally attempt to lodge information within long-term memory, so that it can be remembered later, we engage in *explicit learning*. Explicit learning involves active attention so that material can be encoded. However, what we do at the point of encoding affects what will be encoded and thus what is acquired by long-term memory.

In the early 1970s, Fergus Craik and Robert Lockhart argued that the depth, or level to which we process information determines long-term memory. In their *levels of processing theory*, Craik and Lockhart contended that what we remember is governed by whether we process information in a deep or meaningful way, versus in a shallow, more perceptually based way. The box gives you an idea of what is meant by deep versus shallow processing.

Task 1
Please read the following: BOX
Is this word in capital letters?

Task 2
Does the following word rhyme with DAY? Say.

Task 3
Does the following word fit into the sentence below? Horse.

The ___ was standing in the field.

Task 1 can be achieved purely by visual processing, while Task 2 requires more from you, as you have to devote attention to the different words' sounds. Task 3 asks even more, because you now have to consider meaning to give the correct answer. In terms of levels of processing, Task 1's processing is shallow, or superficial; Task 2's processing is also shallow, while Task 3 involves deep, semantic processing.

Many studies confirmed that deeper processing affected memory (as long as depth was relevant at retrieval), yet a major problem with the theory was that depth had to be inferred – there were no means to measure 'depth' to determine how 'deep' a given level of processing was. On the other hand, the theory raised important questions about the nature of processing and what influences the memorability of an item in long-term memory.

Long-term memory is also influenced by *elaboration, distinctiveness* and *expertise*. Craik and Endel Tulving characterized elaboration as a form of processing that produces an enriched memory trace. Enrichment occurs through the activation of meanings associated with whatever is being represented in memory, and also by linking this representation to a network of interconnected concepts. This means that the memory trace has more retrieval cues, or memory prompts available and thus is more easily accessed from LTM.

ELABORATION

Imagine that you are taking part in a memory experiment in which the stimuli are words. One of the items that you must remember is 'horse'. Which of the following two sentences do you think would lead to 'horse' being better remembered?

(a) The horse was standing in the field.
(b) The chestnut-coloured horse was standing in the field, tail swishing from side to side, as she watched her foal.

The second sentence is more elaborate; more effort goes into processing (b) and it involves richer processing than (a).

A distinctive memory trace is created when an encoded item is processed differently from other similar items and so its representation stands out in LTM. Although the following is an anecdotal example, it nevertheless demonstrates well how distinctiveness contributes to a memory trace. On changing jobs, a new employee reported that they had wanted to be able to quickly put names to the faces of colleagues in the department. Unfortunately, their ability to do so had been hampered by all bar one of the female co-workers possessing similar names: Katherine, Cath, Katie, Katy, Clare, Claire, Katrina, Kay and Scarlett. Scarlett's name proved the easiest to recall and her name was learned first. The similarity of other colleagues' names made them hard to remember because the memory traces created for them were similar. Consequently, at recall, there was competition among the assorted memories. Scarlett's name, however, was so very different, or singular against the other names, that it had a distinctive memory trace which was easy to distinguish and thus easy to access.

Experts on a subject are better at encoding new information on their area of expertise than are novices. An anecdotal example of this comes from two people who unexpectedly saw a steam train. The train was travelling quickly along the track and was viewed at some distance across a field, just before it disappeared behind a line of trees. It was quite impossible to read the name of the engine. One person remarked, 'A steam train!' The second individual commented, 'That's not just a steam train, it's *The Flying Scotsman!*' Despite the train's speed, the expert could encode its appearance rapidly and effectively to allow for its identification as *The Flying Scotsman*.

More rigorous evidence from research has shown that experts in areas such as soccer, American football, baseball, chess, electronic circuits and computer code are all better at encoding new information about these subjects than are novices (see box). Expertise on a topic provides an organizational framework into which new information can be slotted; where this framework isn't present, or not present to the same extent, there is greater difficulty in organizing newly encoded information. Furthermore, expertise also leads to employing distinctive information when encoding, to better encode information which differentiates similar items.

The Flying Scotsman.

EXPERTISE AT PLAYING CHESS:
ADRIAAN DE GROOT'S CLASSIC STUDY
In this famous study, chess grand masters and more novice
players were shown a chess board with the pieces in their
mid-game positions. All participants had only a five-second
glimpse of the pieces' arrangement on the board and then
had to recreate this layout on another chess board. The
grand masters were considerably more successful than the
more novice players. However, when de Groot went on
to present a chess board on which the pieces were placed
randomly, the experts were no better than the novices.

With the board that represented a game position, the
grand masters were able to organize the pieces' positions
in a way that was unavailable to the novices. While the

less-expert players saw the chess pieces as individual items, the masters perceived them as a related whole, in which their relationships were appreciated.

Game of chess.

Not all learning is explicit; some is implicit. There are a number of definitions of *implicit learning*. A simple definition is that it occurs when we learn without being consciously aware that we are doing so. A more thorough description, provided by Arthur S. Reber, contends that implicit learning is a process during which complex knowledge is acquired; it is gained mostly without conscious control and results in the possession of implicit knowledge which is very difficult to express. This can be seen in the acquisition of a first language. In order to be able to use our first language properly, we have to learn its rules; these are picked up over time, such that we gain the knowledge of how language is put together but typically, we'd be hard pressed to explain its rules. Other examples of implicit learning include: music perception, socialization and learning to ride a bike.

Reber has also proposed that particular characteristics differentiate implicit learning from explicit learning. He contended that:

1) *IQ Independence*: Implicit learning is independent of IQ scores; that is, compared with explicit learning, it is relatively unaffected by IQ.

2) *Low Variability*: There is less difference in implicit learning between individuals than there is with explicit learning.

3) *Robustness*: Implicit, unconscious processes are more robust than explicit processes, in terms of disorders such as amnesia,

as they evolved earlier.

4) *Age Independence*: Unlike explicit learning, implicit learning is comparatively unaffected by age and developmental level.

5) *Commonality*: Most species possess implicit systems.

Finally, having made the distinction between explicit and implicit learning, and having devoted space to their differences, it should, of course, be pointed out that learning frequently consists of both.

TYPES OF LONG-TERM MEMORY

Different kinds of long-term memory have been distinguished. Its two main divisions are declarative and nondeclarative memory, with each of these being further subdivided. Declarative memory consists of two subdivisions: episodic and semantic memory. Nondeclarative memory has more subdivisions, but for brevity only procedural memory is discussed below, as this will have greatest familiarity for the reader.

Before going further, please answer the questions in the box.

QUESTIONS
(a) Can you recall where you were and what you were doing this morning or yesterday evening?
(b) When did you last purchase something?
(c) Where is the Statue of Liberty?
(d) Who wrote the detective stories concerning the characters Miss Marple and Hercule Poirot?
(e) Can you drive a car, or ride a bike (that is, you are not a learner)?
(f) Do you play an instrument beyond the level of a learner?

With (a)–(d), did you feel as though you were deliberately seeking the answer from your memory? If your replied yes to (e) and/

or (f) do you get on with the activity or do you think about it? That is, if you are a cyclist, do you get on to your bike and begin pedalling or do you have to actively remember how to ride?

Declarative memory is associated with *consciously* and *explicitly* remembering that something is so. This includes events and facts such as: that I was at the library this morning; that I bought a stamp yesterday; that the Statue of Liberty is in New York harbour and that Agatha Christie wrote about Miss Marple and Hercule Poirot. Nondeclarative memory, on the other hand, involves remembering how to do something like riding a bike or playing the guitar; it is *implicit* and not associated with consciously remembering. Of course, you are not immediately proficient at these kinds of activities but, over time, you become so, such that an experienced guitar player, for example, can pick up the instrument and find chords without actively having to recollect what they must do.

Evidence that declarative and nondeclarative memory are different types of memory comes from people who have amnesia (see box overleaf), in which, while declarative memory is lost, there is evidence for nondeclarative memory being present. This was observed in Henry Molaison, who, for example, could not remember where he lived, that his uncle had died, or where the lawn mower was housed. However, he could recall how to mow a lawn; he learned how to mirror draw, along with acquiring pursuit rotor skills, in which a moving object is tracked. (Further consideration is given to his mirror drawing skills in the discussion of procedural memory on page 118.) In other words, as well as remembering the procedure involved with cutting a lawn, Mr Molaison learned and retained the ability to trace an object – even though he could only see it as a reversed image – and he also learned how to manually track a moving target. Another example comes from Steven Anderson and colleagues, who reported that two experienced drivers with severe amnesia, when tested in a driving simulator and under road conditions, could control their vehicle as well as drivers without brain damage in terms of steering properly, controlling speed, managing driving distraction and avoiding safety errors. These are just two examples of where declarative memory has been lost while nondeclarative memory remains. Many other examples exist, which indicates that the two are different types of long-term memory.

AMNESIA

- The term *amnesia* refers to a temporary or permanent loss of memory resulting from brain damage.
- The kind of amnesia discussed here involves a permanent, profound loss of long-term memory.
- *Retrograde amnesia* refers to an inability to access memories formed before brain damage occurred.
- *Anterograde amnesia* refers to an inability to create new memories subsequent to experiencing brain damage.

Let's now look at declarative memory in more detail. Episodic memory involves memory for *when* and *where* events and experiences have occurred. To quote Endel Tulving, episodic memory makes it possible for us to engage in 'mental time travel': that is, we can go back in time to recreate our previous events and experiences and mentally look forward to future life episodes. However, when we remember past events, memory does not operate like a motion picture in which what was recorded remains exactly the same; instead, we extract the essence of the episode. If you think back to your last visit somewhere, such as to a supermarket or a museum, you won't recall every single episode that took place on that visit but you will have the gist of the experience. Furthermore, your memory will be unlike replaying a film in that episodic memory is *constructive* rather than reproductive.

The earliest research to show that episodic memory is constructive comes from Sir Frederic Bartlett, in work from the early half of the 20th century. Famously, he gave his participants a folk tale to read and later recall entitled *The War of the Ghosts*. This was a Native American story, with cultural ideas unfamiliar to his University of Cambridge students, and their content-recall did not reproduce the original. Among other changes his students made to the folktale, it was altered so that its meaning accorded better with the participants' own cultural perspective.

Bartlett concluded that memory is constructed using *schemas*, or mental frameworks, which are structured according to the cultural and social circumstances in which they are formed. They are employed in three ways: to make sense of new information; to structure and store the information, and to draw upon when remembering. Since the university students' schemas did not fit with the content of *The War of the Ghosts*, the tale was altered to fit with what their schemas led them to expect.

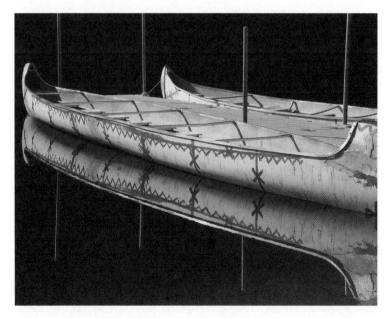

Canoes feature in The War of the Ghosts. *Briefly, the story involves two young men who hear war cries and the sound of paddles. Five men in a canoe ask the young men to join them in making war. One does so but is shot. He realizes he is with ghosts, and on returning home, dies.'*

Unfortunately, aspects of Bartlett's methodology were flawed, but his concept of schema proved sufficiently important to have been regarded as worthy of development. Furthermore, Bartlett's conclusion that memory is constructive has stood the test of time, with various researchers questioning why we have a constructive episodic memory given that this leads to errors? Answers have included that remembering every episodic detail is simply unnecessary and that constructive memory provides flexibility for imagining the future. For example, Daniel Schacter and Donna Addis have argued that in order to think about future events, a reproductive memory would be unhelpful because past and future events, typically, are not identical. In contrast, a constructive memory allows for the gist of what has happened in the past to be remembered and what is remembered can be rearranged to imagine the future.

Semantic memory consists of general knowledge about the world. It is huge because it contains quantities of information across a wide range, such as: the first World War ended in 1918; each molecule of water contains two hydrogen atoms and one oxygen atom; Emily Brontë wrote the novel, *Wuthering Heights*; the meaning of words; Wellington is the capital of New Zealand; Ben Nevis is the highest mountain in the UK; the rules of a given sport. Semantic memories are divorced from the experience of learning, in the sense that we do not remember when and where we acquired the information. For example, are you familiar with the following word and what it means: 'book'? The chances are you replied in the affirmative to both parts of the question but do you remember the time(s) when you learned this information? Or when you learned that books can come in hardback, paperback and electronic formats? Despite not knowing when and where you acquired 'book' you nevertheless have a mental representation or *concept* of the item held within semantic memory.

Eleanor Rosch and colleagues maintained that concepts are organized into hierarchies consisting of three levels. They are, in descending order: the *superordinate*, *basic-level* and *subordinate* categories (see box below). The highest, superordinate category level is the most general; the lowest, subordinate category level is the most specific; while the middle, basic level is neither very general nor very specific but falls between the two. Among many results, Rosch et al. found that the basic level category is the one that is employed most often by adults and it is also the one used initially by children who are developing language skills. It is the most useful level because it simultaneously carries the most information while still allowing for differentiation between items. For example, if discussing musical talent, a person is more likely to say 'I play *piano*', as opposed to 'I play a *musical instrument*', or 'I play a *baby grand piano*', although there are, of course, occasions when the latter two categories can be appropriate. Likewise, a child is more likely to say 'dog' than 'animal' or 'labrador'.

CONCEPT HIERARCHY EXAMPLES			
Category level	Example 1	Example 2	Extent of Specificity
Superordinate	Furniture	Animal	Low
Basic-level	Table	Cat	Medium
Subordinate	Coffee table	Tabby	High

Semantic memories are also held within schemas. A schema holds multiple pieces of information organized into a single unit of knowledge; schemas exist for world knowledge, or facts, people, events and actions. Our schemas are not fixed and static but undergo modification dependent upon our experiences and new information we encounter.

One kind of schema is called a *script*: scripts contain temporally ordered information for interpreting and understanding sequences of events. The most commonly cited example is a restaurant script, which – once you are seated at the table – would include consulting the menu, ordering food, ordering a drink, waiting for the food to be cooked and served, eating it, and paying the bill. Going to a supermarket would involve getting a trolley or basket, taking items from the shelves and placing them in the trolley or basket, queuing if necessary to pay at the checkout, following the routine at the checkout according to whether it is self-service or staff-operated, packing shopping bags and paying. The script helps us know what happens next (such as, once shopping is scanned and bagged, payment must be made before leaving) and what is appropriate (for example, tipping in a restaurant but not at a supermarket).

However, the distinction between episodic and semantic memory is not absolutely clear-cut. Other research has revealed that there is interdependence between the two during encoding and retrieval. Consequently, Daniel Greenberg and Mieke Verfaellie have proposed a typology somewhat different from the classic division. Drawing attention to the way in which memories cannot always be plainly assigned as either episodic or semantic, due to their being a mixture of both, Greenberg and Verfaellie proposed an extra memory type.

In this conceptualization, episodic and semantic memory are deemed to be extremes, with general memories – those memories which have elements of each – existing at some point between the two.

As discussed already, nondeclarative, procedural memory consists of memories for skills. These develop gradually, through repetition. Already mentioned activities such as riding a bike, driving and playing an instrument involve procedural memory. Other procedural memories include tying shoelaces, how to walk, swimming, writing, word processing and mirror drawing. Admittedly, mirror drawing is not a daily activity but it is a good example of acquiring a procedural memory and is one which Henry Molaison was able to achieve.

Mirror drawing involves being presented with a shape which has two outlines and the task is to draw the shape, within the outlines (see opposite) using only what can be seen in a mirror:

that is, the shape itself, the pencil used for drawing, the pencil's marks and your hand. This is quite a tricky exercise, at least initially, as we are not accustomed to drawing with mirror-reflected feedback as to which direction the hand and pencil should take when drawing. Given a five-pointed star to draw, Mr Molaison's efforts were similar to those made by people without a brain impairment: he improved across the ten occasions on which he was asked to draw the star, and he retained the skill well over a three-day period. Of course, due to his inability to form declarative memories, Mr Molaison did not know he was improving, nor did he remember that he had ever done the task before. However, his improved motor (muscle) skill learning for mirror drawing evidenced that procedural memory is a separate kind of memory.

Representation of a five-pointed star for mirror drawing. The task is to trace the shape in the space between the inner star and outer star.

FORGETTING

Forgetting occurs when learned information is not remembered. Different reasons have been supplied for why we forget from short- and long-term memory and only some of these are considered below.

For short-term memory, *decay* and *interference* have been commonly proposed as accounts of forgetting. The decay explanation contends that memory fades in the time between information being acquired and the point at which it must be retrieved. The interference account maintains that earlier items that have been remembered affect memory for later items (*proactive interference*). However, it is unclear which of the two best explains short-term forgetting. On the one hand, various researchers have manipulated the length of time items must be retained, along with how many items have to be remembered during the retention period, with the result that interference yields more forgetting than decay. On the other hand, different researchers using different techniques have concluded that short-term forgetting has a pattern in which there is early, rapid decay, with later forgetting being the product of interference.

Decay cannot adequately account for forgetting from long-term memory, given that many memories of this type are not lost over increasing time. Explanations of forgetting due to interference come in two forms: *proactive interference* and *retroactive interference*. As with short-term memory, proactive interference occurs when previously acquired memories disturb retrieval of new memories. Retroactive interference involves new memories disrupting retrieval of previous memories. In both cases, there is competition between similar memories for retrieval and this leads to forgetting. However, while interference can account for some instances of forgetting, it does not explain all failures to remember.

Interference is, though, related to the consolidation of memories. New memories require strengthening, and John Wixted has argued that this process is affected if mental activity occurs and interferes with their consolidation. In other words, forgetting is caused by a lack of consolidation, which explains why those situations which reduce or eliminate mental activity, such as sleep, improve memory. Subsequent to consolidation, memories become more robust and less susceptible to the effects of interference. Yet, while the lack of consolidation can explain some forgetting, it does not account for the effects of overlap between a memory trace and the circumstances at retrieval.

In his *encoding specificity theory*, Tulving contended that memory is better when there is a good overlap between information held in memory and the information available at retrieval. When the overlap is insufficient, *cue-dependent* forgetting can occur and this can be seen when external and internal contexts differ between encoding and retrieval. An example of the former is found in Duncan Godden and Alan Baddeley's work with regard to training deep sea divers. They discovered that recall was better if the divers learned and recalled in the same context (land-land; underwater-underwater), than if there was a change in learning and recall context (land-underwater; underwater-land). The same principle applies to internal contexts: forgetting is more likely to occur if a person's internal context changes between learning and recall, such as a shift in mood, or a shift in drug- or alcohol-influenced state.

However, cue-dependent forgetting also has limits. It cannot explain recognition failures, since Godden and Baddeley's recall results were not repeated when participants were tested on recognition. Additionally, as James Nairne has pointed out: (1) forgetting may occur because retrieval cues activate the wrong memory, which interferes with accessing the correct information, and (2) daily life produces overlaps with episodes we have experienced previously, yet they do not cause us to have awareness of remembering, as would be expected by Tulving's theory.

Finally, you may be asking whether it is possible to deliberately forget? The answer is yes. Experimentally, it is possible to direct participants to forget certain items and remember others. This is *directed forgetting*. Additionally, in *motivated forgetting*, there exists a motivation to block out traumatic memories.

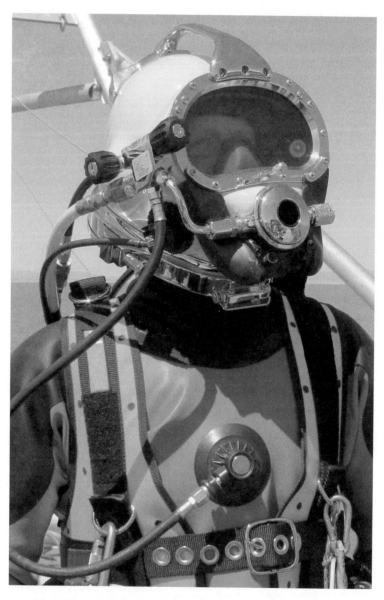

Godden and Baddeley's research concerned the training of deep-sea divers. They found that if the divers' external context (land/underwater) changed between learning and retrieval, recall was poorer than when the context remained the same. Cue-dependent forgetting had occurred.

Key Points

- Remembering involves encoding, storage and retrieval.
- Memory has sensory, short-term and long-term stores. Short- and long-term memory differ in capacity, duration and the preferred form of encoding with visually presented, verbal material.
- Working memory (STM) consists of the central executive, visuo-spatial sketchpad, phonological loop and episodic buffer.
- LTM memories are acquired explicitly and implicitly.
- Depth of processing, elaboration, distinctiveness and expertise affect LTM.
- LTM consists of declarative – episodic and semantic – memories plus nondeclarative memories, e.g., procedural memory.
- STM forgetting is associated with decay and interference; LTM forgetting explanations include: interference, cue-dependent forgetting, directed forgetting and motivated forgetting.

Chapter 5

Language

Although there are many languages in the world, much language research has concentrated upon English. Different languages do not operate in exactly the same ways, thus what follows, though it applies to English, may not automatically apply to other languages.

Language is everywhere in life. Its heard, spoken, written and read forms are such a major means of communication that it is hard to imagine a world without language. Of course, the spoken and heard word can vary from being quite fleeting, to involving lengthy discussions; communication may be face-to-face, over the phone, or we may be listening to and/or watching one of various media. The written word, too, may be brief: perhaps involving reading just a note; information on a ticket, or in an advertising poster, or else be longer in a magazine or book. Although letters are less frequent now, education involves producing written material, often at length, and emails and text messages have to be composed. Indeed, language is such a major means of communication, and is so fundamental to life, that the stages of language acquisition are major developmental milestones. Moreover, language's loss, in whatever form, can lead to a serious impact upon the person it affects.

THE COMPONENTS OF LANGUAGE

There are a number of different components to language. These are outlined in the box beneath – which can be used as a memory aid – and then discussed in more detail.

LANGUAGE

Language = words + rules (which govern how words may be used to express meaning).

Words – consist of phonemes.

Phonemes – are the individual sounds of a language and combine to produce morphemes.

Morphemes – are the smallest meaningful units of language.

Grammar – the rules of using words meaningfully. Grammar consists of semantics and syntax.

Semantics – the application of meaning to morphemes and words.

Syntax – the rules of how to form and structure a sentence.

Language consists of words and rules, with the rules determining how words must be employed for meaning to be expressed. The words in a language consist of *phonemes*, or the individual sounds of a given language. Say the following words – 'eight' and 'ate'; these are two quite different words but their phonemes are the same. 'Late' and 'date' share the same phonemes apart from each word's initial sound, which is sufficient to make the words' meanings different. The words 'ethics' and 'either' share a 'th' combination but the sound of the letters' combination is different in the two words. We can see a phonemic difference too, in the pronunciation of the word 'loch'; English people typically give the 'ch' a harder sound than Scots, such that 'loch' is pronounced in the same way as 'lock'.

Phonemes combine to produce *morphemes,* the smallest meaningful units of language. The word 'reach', for instance, consists of one morpheme but 'unreachable' consists of three morphemes: un + reach + able. Other morphemes include: anti-, dis-, pre-; -er, -ist, -ly, as well as the past tense -ed and the plural -s.

Grammar relates to the rules of using words meaningfully and it comprises semantics, (associating meaning with morphemes and words), along with *syntax* (the rules of sentence formation and structure).

SPEECH PRODUCTION

Saying something does not begin with words. Instead, we begin with semantics, or the meaning of what is to be said and the concept to be expressed, which is typically planned and produced on a clause-by-clause basis.

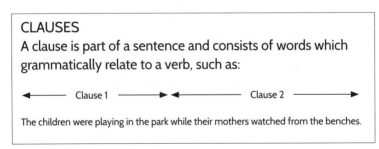

CLAUSES
A clause is part of a sentence and consists of words which grammatically relate to a verb, such as:

◄──── Clause 1 ────►◄──── Clause 2 ────►

The children were playing in the park while their mothers watched from the benches.

A general structure of what is to be communicated is formed: syntax (grammar, word order) is established. What has been formulated in terms of morphemes (vocabulary) must be turned into phonemes which are then articulated. Articulation involves messages being sent to relevant muscles which control the mouth so that the tongue, lips and teeth are in the correct place for the phonemes to be produced correctly. Prosody (emphasis, intonation, rhythm) is required too. It is unusual for us to think about how we articulate language: the simple exercises in the box below are designed to help with this. A prosody exercise is supplied too.

PRODUCING SOUNDS AND PROSODY

Producing Sounds

1) Put the palm of your hand a few centimetres away from your mouth and say the word 'push'. What are your lips doing? What do you feel on the palm of your hand?

2) Say the word 'mean' – are your lips doing something different from in (1)?

3) Say 'tank' – what is happening with your tongue?

Prosody

4) Say the following, emphasizing each time the word in italics:

(a) the *boy's* jumper   (b) the boy's *jumper*

The emphasis placed on a given word draws attention to a specific element of what is said. Emphasis, intonation and rhythm help us to communicate clearly.

When speech is produced, it is fluent but not continuous in the sense that there are pauses present. Pauses occur for different reasons. These include, for example: a signal that this is the point at which another person can take their turn to speak; that a person is searching for a particular word to fully accurately convey meaning; and to create a dramatic effect. The latter may be observed in the kind of television show where a competitor or competitors are excluded from one episode of the show to the next – *'leaving us tonight are [prolonged pause] …'*. Importantly, though, pauses also indicate that planning occurs in clauses: pauses are commonly found at the boundary between one clause and another. When the pause occurs, planning of the following clause is taking place.

Another indicator that speech is planned in clauses comes from *slips of the tongue,* or speech errors. Two kinds of errors that people make are called *word exchange* and *root morpheme exchange* errors. Suppose you intended to say 'a piece of pie' but made a slip, saying instead, 'a pie of piece'; in this case, a word exchange error has been made because two words have swapped their places. On the other hand, if the intended expression was 'the arms of a shirt' but 'the shirts of an arm' was said instead, this would be a *root morpheme exchange*. That is, the roots 'arm' and 'shirt' exchanged but the plural morpheme (or, more technically, the *inflection*) 's' stayed in position. These kinds of slips frequently occur within, rather than between clauses; hence, speech must be planned at the clause-level.

Other speech errors arise too, and these also provide evidence for how speech is planned. Sometimes, an intended word is replaced by a different one and the different word can share a similar concept or sound:

Intended: 'she arrived too early'.   Error: 'she arrived too late'.
Intended: 'don't take that attitude'. Error: 'don't take that altitude'.

These slips indicate that the mental lexicon, or dictionary associated with language is organized according to both meaning (early/late belong to the same concept: time), and sound ('attitude' and 'altitude' though different in meaning sound similar).

A well-known speech error is the Spoonerism, named after the Reverend W. Spooner, who supposedly commonly made this kind of slip:

Intended: 'you have missed all my history lectures'.
Error: 'you have hissed all my mystery lectures'.

Spoonerisms involve the reversal of either two consonant phonemes or two vowel phonemes. The sounds are similar and may occur across nouns, adjectives and verbs. Typically, Spoonerisms occur within clauses, which adds to the evidence that the clause is a planning unit. However, this sort of slip also shows that speech planning takes place before articulation and that words are not planned phoneme to phoneme. 'Missed' and 'history' must both have existed as groups of phonemes for the 'h' and 'm' sounds to have exchanged.

The earlier root morpheme exchange, 'the shirts of the arm' (error), instead of 'the arms of the shirt' (intended) tells us something else, too. Say them both out loud and note what happens to the plural 's' in 'shirts' and 'arms'. With this error, the inflection's sound fits the root morpheme exchange, so it must have been added after the root morphemes exchanged.

Of course, when we speak, we are communicating something to other people. Yet everyone is not the same, and what is said must be appropriate to whoever is our audience. There must be *common ground* for communication to be successful. Common ground helps different speakers to understand each other, yet this is not automatically present – it must be established. Suppose you were to hear the expression 'it's parky'. If you share common ground with the speaker, you would know that this is a reference to the weather and that it is cold. However, if the speaker has not established common ground, upon hearing the expression you would look blank and they would have to establish it by clarifying that what has been said was a remark about the coldness of the weather. Common ground may not be shared by professionals (who are experts in their own area, such as lawyers) and those of us who do not possess similar expertise. In this case, the professional must adjust their terminology so that it fits with the other person's level of knowledge and understanding.

Reverend William Spooner.

THEORIES OF WORD PRODUCTION IN SPEECH

Two well-known theories of word production are going to be discussed. One is Gary S. Dell's interactive, spreading activation model; the other is known as WEAVER++ from the work of Willem Levelt and colleagues and the work of Ardi Roelofs.

In Dell's model, word production involves three layers of units, or nodes. At the top, there are the semantic nodes, beneath these the word nodes, and then finally, on the bottom layer, the phoneme nodes. The semantic nodes represent the features of what it is you wish to convey. If this happens to be 'dog', for instance, then certain of the semantic nodes associated with this could be 'mammal' and 'barks'; on the other hand, if you wish to convey 'bird', semantic nodes would include 'feathers' and 'beak'. Once a semantic representation is active, this activation goes on to spread through the network, that is, *spreading activation* occurs. For a word to be produced, first, the right word must be retrieved, followed by the retrieval of its phonemes. The *interactive* nature of the model results from word-semantic information affecting the retrieval of phonemes, and phonological information affecting word retrieval.

In Dell's model, semantic nodes represent the features of what it is you wish to convey. If this is 'bird', relevant semantic nodes would include 'feathers' and 'beak'.

Let's suppose it is 'dog' that you wish to convey. A jolt of activation is received by the relevant semantic nodes and it spreads. Activation occurs in those word nodes which possess characteristics associated with the idea you want to convey. This means that the 'dog' word node will be activated along with other semantically related words, such as 'doggy', 'puppy', 'mongrel', 'wolf', 'cat', and so forth. (A cat is also a mammal and has a tail etc.) While this is occurring, the phonemes which are shared by other words which possess the same sounds as 'dog' – dig, dip, fog, clog, blog, for example – send activation upwards to the word nodes. The word node that ultimately receives the greatest activation, in this case 'dog', will be selected for use.

Dogs. According to Dell's model, saying the word 'dog' will involve semantic nodes, word nodes and phoneme nodes.

When you are ready to speak the word 'dog', its word node will receive an activation jolt.

This allows for 'dog' now to be fitted into a sentence, so long as it belongs to the correct syntactic class. That is, the sentence that you are going to speak will possess an expected syntactic structure. This specifies, for instance, that a noun is needed in a particular place and a verb in another, as in: *the dog sat*. Here, after *the*, a noun is required followed by a verb. If 'dog' fits with the expected syntactic class – noun – then it can be slotted into the sentence. Once the word node has received its jolt, activation travels to the phoneme layer. Those phonemes with the greatest activation are selected, in this case the individual sounds which make 'dog'.

The name of the second model, WEAVER++, is an acronym for *W*ord *E*ncoding by *A*ctivation and *Ver*ification. It is similar to Dell's model in that it also involves three layers, along with spreading activation, and two stages to word production. However, as we shall see, there are differences, too.

From top to bottom, the three layers of word production are (1) the concept, (2) *lemma* and (3) word-form levels. Concept nodes represent the whole of a concept such as 'dog', 'tree' or 'car'. Lemma nodes are concerned with syntax. Lemmas represent the syntactic properties of a word, such as its syntactic class (noun, verb, etc.); its tense (present, past, future, etc.); number (single/ plural); first, second or third person; and the gender of words in those languages in which words possess gender, such as French and German. (In French, for example, the word for tree, *arbre* is masculine whilst the word for leaf, *feuille* is feminine.) The word-form layer involves morpheme, phoneme and phonetic nodes. As their names imply, these produce the necessary morphemes, phonemes and the necessary responses for articulating a word.

In terms of the connections between the three layers, there is a two-way connection between the concept nodes and lemma nodes. Activation not only spreads downwards from concepts but also upwards from lemmas. The connection between concept nodes and lemma nodes serves another purpose too: it carries information as to how the nodes are related, for example that the lemma for *dog* represents the concept 'dog'. After the lemma level, however, activation spreads in one direction only – downwards – once the relevant lemma has been accessed.

More concretely, let's suppose that you again want to articulate the concept 'dog', which necessitates that the *dog* lemma is accessed. As this is attempted, activation spreads from the concept 'dog' to related concepts ('puppy', 'mongrel', 'cat', etc.) and to the lemma nodes (*dog, puppy, mongrel, cat,* etc.) Activation spreads upwards too, from lemma nodes to concept nodes due to their two-way connection. If the *dog* lemma node's activation reaches a high enough level to rule out the competition from other active lemma nodes, then it is selected, providing that it accurately represents the concept to be expressed.

Selection of the *dog* lemma means that syntactic information is available: the word is a noun and singular. This information is now sent onwards to produce the appropriate word form. At the morpheme level, the stem morpheme DOG is produced. Next, the phoneme level uses the stem morpheme information to establish the phonological segments of DOG, so that they can be turned into syllables. DOG, of course, has one syllable; had the appropriate stem morpheme been PUPPY, though, its phonological segments would have resulted in two syllables. Once the number of syllables has been established, they are supplied with a stress pattern and all the information from the phoneme nodes is sent to the phonetic nodes. Here, phonetic programmes deliver the articulation required to produce the word 'dog'.

The verification part of the account involves self-monitoring. That is, the speaker monitors their speech production so that errors are typically detected before they are produced.

SPEECH PERCEPTION

Given that speech production involves the articulation of phonemes, it is probably unsurprising that speech perception requires the detection of phonemes and determining which phonemes belong together and constitute words. Although we do this every day when holding conversations, listening to what is being said on radio, TV, streaming services, or in the cinema or theatre, it is not unusual for speech to be competing with other sounds. For example, in the cinema and theatre people cough and may make noises with sweet wrappers. If you meet a friend outside, on a busy street, their speech must be perceived from among the different sounds around you, such as building work, traffic, other people's conversations, and so on.

When we hear speech, the ability to identify separate words is affected by whether we are familiar with the language or not. If English is your first language, then detecting the different words in spoken English appears easy, yet if you overhear another conversation, in a language you do not know well, individual words cannot be separated from what seems like a flow of sounds. Yet, despite the apparent ease you experience in perceiving sounds in your first language, your speech perception is coping with various issues while this happens.

Speech is not identical from person to person. Using English as an example, speakers who have English as a first language differ in their accents according to country and region. A classic example of the pronunciation of English words being affected by a country's accent is found in the way in which 'fish and chips' is said. In Great Britain, 'fish' would be pronounced *fish* and 'chips' *chips*; in Australia, though, the pronunciation is *feesh* and *cheeps,* while in New Zealand it is *fush* and *chups*. However, it is unlikely that people from Australia, Britain or New Zealand would struggle to understand these pronunciation differences.

That within a country, different accents lead to different phonemes being used in words is seen in the pronunciation of 'bath'. Some people in the UK pronounce the vowel with a shorter sound and others with a longer sound. That is, 'bath' where the 'a' is sounded like the 'a' in 'attitude', versus a pronunciation akin to 'barth'.

Other issues that have to be dealt with when perceiving speech are that people speak at different speeds and voice qualities differ, such as higher versus deeper voices. Moreover, even when the same person is speaking, phonemes alter in sound as a result of *coarticulation*. This refers to the way in which speech sounds can be affected by a preceding or subsequent phoneme. For example, say the single word 'mat' and notice the vowel sound of the 'a'. Now say the single word 'cat' and again notice the 'a' sound. Can you hear the way in which the vowel sound is nasal in 'mat' but not 'cat'? Here is a different example: say the single word 'pen' and then the word 'pet'. Can you hear how the sound associated with the vowel is nasal in the former?

How, then, do we determine which sound combinations yield words, given that there are so many variations in the speech that we hear? Factors that help with this include coarticulation, which provides word boundary information because it happens more commonly within word boundaries than from one word to the next. Knowledge of a language helps too, since we know what can legitimately constitute a word and what cannot. Knowledge can also be employed in conjunction with context information to determine what has been said. Suppose that you are in the cinema and somebody coughs so that you miss something that a character has said; or you are outside and a road drill starts up and you miss a segment of what your friend was saying. The context of what has been said can be used to work out what has been lost.

The effects of context information were demonstrated by Richard Warren and Roslyn Warren, who gave their participants a listening task in which a single phoneme was replaced by a cough, as in our cinema example. All participants heard exactly the same sentence apart from the final word. The sentence was:

'It was found that the [cough sound] -eel was on the __.'

The final word was one of table, axle, shoe and orange. Accordingly, participants reported that they had heard a word which fitted the context of the sentence: table led to meal; axle to wheel; shoe to heel and orange to peel.

How do we recognize words that we hear? Different models of auditory word recognition have been proposed. A well-known account was forwarded by William Marslen-Wilson and colleagues, which, over time, has been redeveloped from its original conceptualization.

MARSLEN-WILSON AND COLLEAGUES'
COHORT MODEL

Originally, it was proposed that when a word is heard, its early sound establishes the *word-initial cohort*. If the first sound is *a* as in 'abstract', 'abacus', 'account' and 'announce', then these words and others which begin with the same sound become activated. As further sounds are heard beyond *a*, these allow words to be eliminated which do not fit the later sound pattern. Consequently, if the next sound leads to *ab*, 'account' and 'announce' are eliminated but 'abstract' and 'abacus' remain, along with any other words which match the *ab* sound pattern. If the next piece of information leads to *aba*, 'abstract' can be eliminated too, and so on, until one word remains – let's say 'abacus'.

In addition to filtering by sound, filtering can also occur if a word is compatible with the syntactic or semantic context. If what you hear is: 'He was performing a calculation using an a_', then the context will help filter out certain words and assist with the selection of the correct word: 'abacus'.

More recent adjustments to the model include amendments to the word-initial cohort and the effects of context. That is, the word-initial cohort is deemed broader, also constituting words where the first phoneme is similar to the one heard and a word's membership status within the cohort is not either exclusively present or absent. Instead, it is conceived that words possess different levels of activation such that the cohort depends on how active a word is.

Another factor facilitating speech perception is the visual information we acquire from looking at a face. In the 1930s, J.C. Cotton had a soundproof booth constructed with a double glass window in its front. The booth's lighting was manipulated so that the face of a person sitting in the booth was either seen or unseen. When the individual behind the window spoke, what they said could not be heard by listeners without the aid of a microphone and a loudspeaker, and different techniques were used to distort the speech so that it was difficult to perceive. When the speaker's face was unseen, Cotton reported that listeners found the speech virtually unintelligible; yet, when listeners could see the speaker's face, they could understand what was being said. Evidently, visual information compensated for the lack of adequate auditory information.

The McGurk Effect also highlights how speech perception is determined by both auditory and visual information. However, as this phenomenon was discussed in more detail in the chapter on *Perception,* only a quick reminder is provided here. Briefly, when 'ba' was seen to be said but 'ga' was heard, participants perceived that what was spoken was 'da'. That 'da' was heard indicates that auditory and visual speech information are combined to produce speech perception. Moreover, this combination occurs before we are consciously aware of what is being said.

Although people may speak using a single word, or just a few words, they commonly speak in sentences. Sentences consist of clauses and phrases (see box overleaf) and syntactic and grammatical rules govern how sentences are formed. Hence, the listener uses this information to understand what has been said. For example, in the simple sentence, 'the girl helped the boy', it is the word order which tells you who is helping whom. If 'girl' and 'boy' are swapped, the sentence has a different meaning. More technically, the sentence has to be *parsed,* or analysed for structure. In a more complex sentence such as, 'the tall girl quickly helped the little boy', it is necessary to parse the adjectives 'tall' and 'little'; the adverb, 'quickly'; and in both sentences, the

'-ed' which informs us about the verb's tense. More information on parsing can be found in the 'Reading' section of this chapter.

PHRASES

A phrase is a group of words which produce a meaningful conceptual unit, such as 'the lion'.

Using the *prosody* (rhythm, intonation and stress) of speech helps assist with a listener's understanding of what is said. *Rhythm* relates to the timing of what is said and helps the listener group words together appropriately. For example, if you were to hear the following sentence rather than read it, the speaker would slow down towards the comma and pause briefly: 'They fixed the ferry in time for me to get to the wedding, it was such a relief.'

Intonation produces changes in the pitch of the speaker's voice. Suppose that on two quite separate occasions you hear the words 'it's very cold'. The first speaker's pitch falls at the end of what is said whereas the second speaker's pitch rises. The same words may have been said but their interpretation would be different: in the first case the listener would take them as a statement, while in the second case they would be understood as a question.

Stress applies emphasis to what is said. In the following examples, the italicized word is the one which is being stressed; if you say (a)–(d) aloud, stressing the words as indicated, it will not only give you an idea of how a speaker uses prosody but also of the information a listener detects. Typically, stressed words are produced differently, such as being spoken slowly and carefully. The examples are: (a) 'A *man* stood on the bridge'; (b) 'A man *stood* on the bridge'; (c) 'A man stood on *the* bridge'; (d) 'A man stood on the *bridge*'. In each case, when the listener hears the stressed word, it is clear which element of the speech is important. That is: (a) it is significant that the person is a man rather than a woman, girl or boy; (b) the individual was standing rather than crossing the bridge; (c) a particular bridge is being referred to; and (d) that the man's position was on the bridge rather than somewhere else. Here is a more comedic example of prosody in action:

PROSODY: *MURDER, SHE WROTE* AND *GHOSTS*

Listeners use prosody to understand speech. The title of the 1980s–90s TV detective series *Murder, She Wrote* is usually said in such a way that the word 'she' is not emphasized. In the BBC comedy, *Ghosts,* however, the Edwardian ghost, Lady Button, delivers the title as Murder, *She* Wrote. The emphasis is on 'she' and this word has a longer duration than 'wrote'. Although this is for comedic effect, from Lady Button's prosody, the listener understands that for her, what is important is that the writer is female.

Angela Lansbury, who starred in Murder, She Wrote.

Accessing meaning from what is spoken is completed in a number of ways. One of these is through *common ground*, or shared knowledge, which was discussed previously. Here, though, are some more examples which demonstrate that a listener's knowledge affects the meaning which is gleaned from speech. The British expression 'it's brass monkeys' is never meant to refer literally to metallic monkeys; instead, the expression is usually understood to mean that the weather is extremely cold. Similarly, if you were in Glasgow and heard the expression 'I'll clap your dog', this does not mean the animal is about to receive a round of applause but that it is about to receive a pat.

Another contributor to meaning is *context*, such as whether a reference to 'beans' most sensibly relates to something eaten or to coffee beans; or whether the way in which words are spoken indicate they are to be taken seriously or humorously. Meaning is acquired too by making *inferences* about what has been said. If you were to hear 'Juanita flew to Chile on Saturday', you would infer that Juanita took an aeroplane, even though this is not explicitly stated. Here, general, or world knowledge allows the listener to elaborate upon what was heard. Likewise, if you heard, 'I looked through the window and quickly dashed to get the washing in', it would be likely inferred that the cause of this action was that it was raining. Here, an inference is drawn between what is being stated now – 'quickly dashed to get the washing in' – and what came before – 'I looked through the window'. Inferences can be made based on one word alone, such as 'spinster', which today is understood to mean a single woman of a certain age who has never been married and is a term that typically attracts negative connotations. (This inference contrasts markedly with the word's original meaning, which referred to a woman who was able to support herself and be independent by spinning wool.)

WRITING

Compared with having a conversation, writing frequently provides a more permanent form of communication. Historic manuscripts,

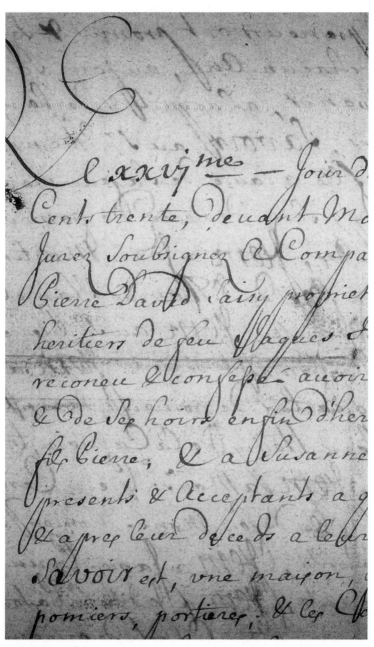

A manuscript letter.

for example, were handwritten on papyrus, parchment, vellum and paper and are, centuries later, still available for inspection. Without the written word it would be impossible to know if certain works, such as Shakespeare's plays, are being delivered verbatim, as per the First Folio of 1623. Indeed, writing is an essential life skill without which essays, emails, job applications, and so forth cannot be created.

Like speaking, writing necessitates several factors: establishing the meaning of what is to be expressed; planning; and generating phrases, clauses and sentences. However, rather than producing speech sounds, writing involves the creation of words on a page or screen by means of handwriting or typing. Other differences between speaking and writing exist too. You are more likely to be on your own when you write; speaking has fewer planning opportunities; conversations involve immediate and ongoing feedback from listeners, whereas writing involves either no feedback, or feedback that is delayed. The written word is revised more regularly than the spoken word, and it is often more formal, with longer, more complex sentences and vocabulary.

MODELS OF WRITING

In the early 1980s, a model of how writing proceeds was proposed by Linda Flower and John Hayes. Over time, changes to this conceptualization have been made. Despite this, it is useful to consider the earlier model first. This is not only because of the impact of Flower and Hayes' original work but is also due to the original model's help in understanding its later formulation in Hayes' model.

Flower and Hayes contended that writing involves distinct thinking processes which can occur at any time when composing written material. Essentially, the writer must integrate a number of issues: planning, remembering, writing and rereading.

The model has three units: the *task environment, long term memory* and *writing processes*. The writing process is influenced by, and influences, the task environment and the writer's

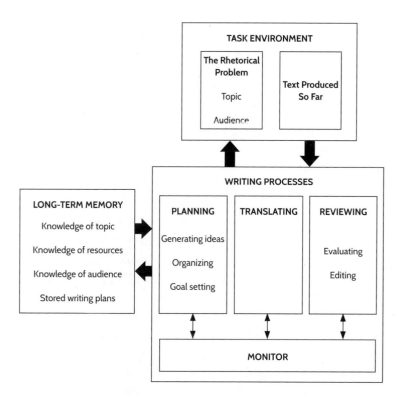

Flower and Hayes' model of writing.

long-term memory. Task environment comprises factors such as: what is being written about; who is receiving the written work, i.e., its audience; the writer's goals in writing; and, once some text has been written, this too influences the writing process. Long-term memory includes information about the audience, the topic under consideration and writing plans. It relates to the writer's own memory, as well as those resources upon which the writer can draw, such as articles and books.

The writing processes constitute *planning, translating* and *reviewing,* which are controlled by a *monitor.* When planning, generated ideas from long-term memory may be already sufficiently well-developed and organized to permit writing. If this is not the case then organization facilitates meaningful writing. The goals created by the writer also play a role in planning. Translating is the process by which ideas are put into visible language, while reviewing subsumes *evaluating* and *revising* what has been written. Finally, the monitor controls the point at which the writer moves from one process to another. That is, the monitor captures differences between writers in terms of how they arrange planning and writing. Some people, for example, prefer to plan and then write while others plan-write, plan-write etc. as they go along.

In his later model, Hayes distinguished three levels involved in writing: the *control level, process level* and *resource level*. The control level comprises *motivation, goal setting* (planning, writing, revising), the *current plan* and *writing schemas*. Motivation affects whether or not a person writes; the amount of time they devote to writing and the extent to which attention is given to the quality of what is produced. Goal setting is associated with planning, writing and revision, while writing schemas are frameworks for writing tasks such as summarizing, revising, collaborating, and so on. Although conceived as being part of the control level, writing schemas are stored in long-term memory.

The resource level involves attention, working memory, long-term memory and reading. (A brief reminder of working memory is provided in the box overleaf.) The process level consists of two parts – the *writing processes* and *task environment*. There are four writing processes: the *proposer, translator, transcriber* and *evaluator,* which overlap with each other. The proposer generates ideas as a result of considering the plan and the information applicable to the plan. The translator converts ideas into 'new language', or new words, by utilizing both long-term memory and working memory (see box). Information from the translator is then changed into text by the transcriber. The fourth writing process, the evaluator, assesses what has been produced and revises it as required.

Finally, the task environment has four parts, three of which affect writing processes. If the writer is working in association

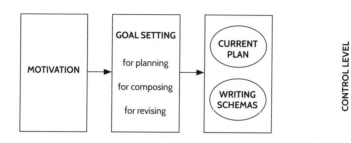

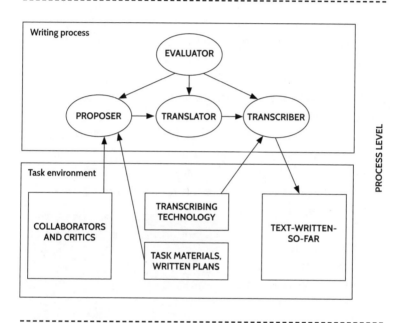

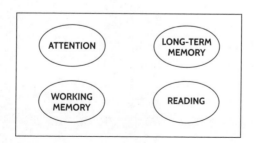

Hayes' model of writing.

with *collaborators* and *critics*, then this affects the proposer, as do *task materials* and *written plans*. Additionally, the transcriber is affected by *transcribing technology* and it also influences the task environment in terms of what has been written so far.

MEMORY AND WRITING
Long-Term Memory

Flower and Hayes pointed out that long-term memory contains knowledge concerning: the topic under discussion; the audience that will read the material; representations of how what is to be written about can be addressed; and writing plans.

For example, the audience under consideration for the kind of writing found in a professional psychology journal is not the same kind of audience as those who would read say, Dame Hilary Mantel's trilogy about the Tudor figure Thomas Cromwell. Both kinds of writing are evidence based, but the former is a strictly scientific report for fellow professionals, while the latter is a work of fiction based on historical evidence.

A psychology paper submitted for publication in a journal must follow a specific rubric: abstract, introduction, methodology, results, discussion references, appendices. An experienced researcher will recall this when writing, along with the accepted academic style. A student who is learning the skill of

Hilary Mantel.

report-writing often has to check to be certain of what material should go where, and they will have less familiarity with the appropriate academic style. Additionally, there will be a difference in knowledge level regarding the topic of a report between the experienced researcher versus a student.

Working Memory

Here is a brief reminder of three of working memory's components:

- *Central Executive* – involved in attention, planning, integrating information from working memory's components.
- *Phonological Loop* – stores sounds briefly; permits verbal rehearsal (repetition).
- *Visuo-Spatial Sketchpad* – responsible for visual and spatial processing.

Writing requires attention which involves the central executive, as do planning, transforming words to text, reading and revision. The phonological loop is required for putting ideas into words, reading what has been written so far and correcting text. The visuo-spatial sketchpad plays a role too in the planning and correcting stages of writing.

NB: Long-term memory and working memory are covered in detail in Chapter 4

READING

As you are reading this text in English, you may be assuming that your eyes are tracking smoothly from left to right across the page, since English reads left to right. However, this is not so: the eyes move in rapid jumps called *saccades* accompanied by *fixations*. Saccades were observed by the French ophthalmologist Louis Emile Javal in the late 19th century, and the word saccade

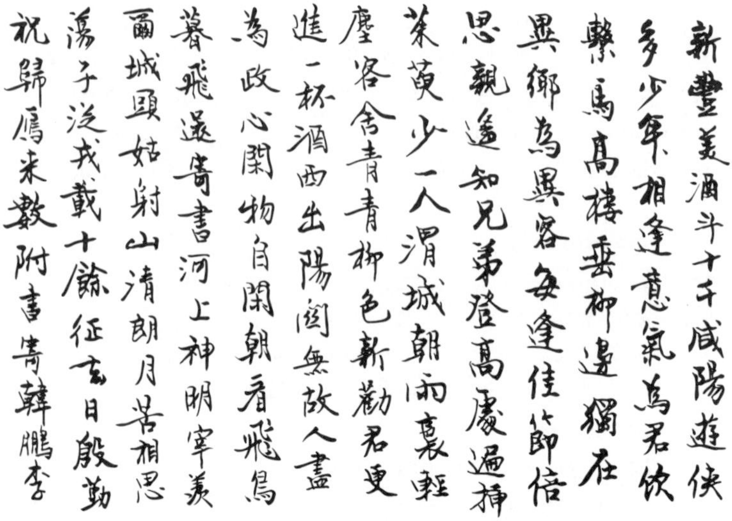

新豐美酒斗十千咸陽遊俠
多少年相逢意氣為君飲
繫馬高樓垂柳邊獨在
興鄉為興客每逢佳節倍
思親遙知兄弟登高處遍插
茱萸少一人渭城朝雨裛輕
塵客舍青青柳色新勸君更
進一杯酒西出陽關無故人畫
為政心閑物自閑朝看飛鳥
暮飛還寄書河上神明宰羨
爾城頭姑射山清朗月苦相思
湯子泛戎戴十餘征玄日殷勤
祝歸鴈來數附書寄韓鵬李

Chinese and Hebrew text.

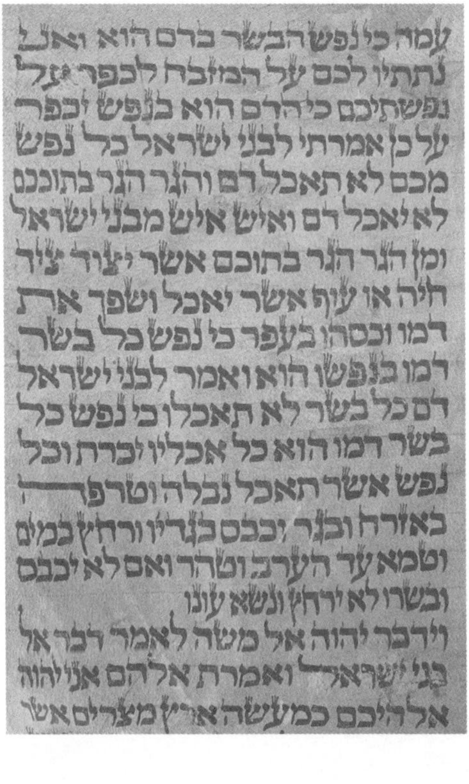

עמה כי נפש הבשר בדם הוא ואני
נתתיו לכם על המזבח לכפר על
נפשתיכם כי הדם הוא בנפש יכפר
על כן אמרתי לבני ישראל כל נפש
מכם לא תאכל דם והגר הגר בתוככם
לא יאכל דם ואיש איש מבני ישראל
ומן הגר הגר בתוכם אשר יציד ציד
חיה או עוף אשר יאכל ושפך את
דמו וכסהו בעפר כי נפש כל בשר
דמו בנפשו הוא ואמר לבני ישראל
דם כל בשר לא תאכלו כי נפש כל
בשר דמו הוא כל אכליו יכרת וכל
נפש אשר תאכל נבלה וטרפה
באזרח ובגר וכבס בגדיו ורחץ במים
וטמא עד הערב וטהר ואם לא יכבס
ובשרו לא ירחץ ונשא עונו
וידבר יהוה אל משה לאמר דבר אל
בני ישראל ואמרת אלהם אני יהוה
אלהיכם כמעשה ארץ מצרים אשר

is French, as used in the expression *advancer par saccades,* which means to move forward jerkily.

The speed of saccades is 20–30 milliseconds (thousandths of a second), covering eight letters/spaces. The majority of saccades are forwards but others – *regressions* – are backwards, to permit refixation when people realize they have missed the meaning of what they have read. When a jump occurs, the eyes land on words rather than spaces.

Information is taken in during fixations of 200–250 milliseconds, 80 per cent of which are on content words (nouns, verbs) and 20 per cent on function words, such as 'the'. Words that are shorter in length or are predictable are jumped over. Up to 15 letters are detected to the right of a fixation and three to four letters to the left, though this can be affected by the size of what is being read and the difficulty of the material. Where material is found to be more challenging, saccades are smaller.

Of course, not all languages read left to right. Hebrew, for example, reads right to left. In this case, the greater number of letters is detected to the left rather than the right of a fixation. Reading Chinese – a logographic language, where single symbols can represent entire words or even concepts – consists of smaller saccades, with two to three characters being detected to the right and one to the left.

An early and highly influential computer simulation of four-letter word recognition was proposed in 1981 by James McClelland and David Rumelhart. This account contended that a written word is processed at three different levels, each of which has recognition units. The levels are the: *feature level*; *letter level* and *word level.*

At the feature level, the features of individual letters are detected and this information goes on to activate feature recognition units. For example, if a vertical line is detected to the left of a letter, as in D, H, R, the feature recognition unit sends activation to the letter recognition units that possess a vertical line to the left, (D, H, R, plus all other letters with

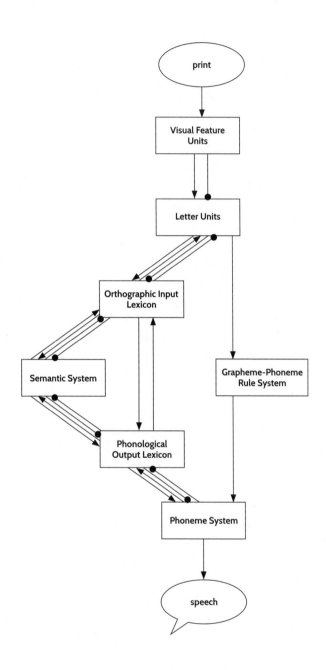

Dual Route Cascaded model.

this feature). Additionally, letter recognition units without this feature are inhibited.

At the letter level, letter recognition units identify individual letters, such as R. Activation is sent to all word recognition units containing an R in the relevant position within a word: for example, in ROPE and RACE, the letter is in the first position, while in PART and CARD, the letter is in the third position. Inhibition is sent to non-relevant word recognition units.

Word recognition itself occurs at the word level. ROPE and RACE would both be activated by R and E as they begin and end with these letters. If the word to be read is RACE, though, ROPE would be inhibited by A and C.

Another approach to reading is the *Dual Route Cascaded* model by Max Coltheart and colleagues. This is a computer model which captures the pronunciation of a printed word in terms of two routes – the direct pathway and the indirect pathway. The direct route is entirely visual: sight of a word alone allows its pronunciation to be accessed. The indirect route, on the other hand, involves sounding-out the word.

Pronunciation of a written word by the direct route proceeds as follows: Once the word has been seen, let's say 'book', it is responded to first by *visual feature units* and then *letter units*, after which the *orthographic lexicon* is accessed. The orthographic lexicon holds the written form of words known to the reader and 'book' will be found in here. The word can now go on to be pronounced by means of the *phonological lexicon* (which holds the pronunciation of words known to the reader) and the *phoneme system*. As the orthographic lexicon and phonological lexicon are connected to the *semantic system*, this allows for the word's meaning to be accessed.

Using the indirect route to read and pronounce a written word again first involves responses from the visual feature units and the letter units. Next, the word's pronunciation is assembled so that it can be spoken. This is achieved through both the *grapheme-phoneme rule system*, which transforms the word's visual representation into its phonemes, or individual sounds, and the *phoneme system*.

'Book' was chosen as the example on page 153 because it is a word that will be known to you. However, let's suppose the following three words are unknown to you, in their written forms: 'yacht', 'subtle' and 'library'. Since the written forms of the words are unknown, they will not be held in your orthographic lexicon; thus, the indirect route for reading and pronunciation must be adopted. 'Library' should present no problem in that it has regular spelling-to-sound correspondences. When its pronunciation is assembled it will be li + bra + ry. Even though you have not seen the word before, you may have heard it. If this is so, its combination of sounds produced by the indirect route will allow for its meaning to be accessed.

'Yacht' and 'subtle' are different from 'library', though, as they possess irregular spelling-to-sound correspondences. Try pretending you really do not know the words and sound them out: the results will be 'ya-chet' and 'sub-tul'. Clearly, these are not the correct pronunciations of the words. Now, even if you are familiar with their correct spoken form and their associated meanings, the indirect route will not allow you to access this information. In marked contrast, when 'yacht' and 'subtle' are known words, the direct route is very effective in accessing the words and their meanings.

The Dual Route Cascaded model's two routes can be seen in how those with *acquired dyslexia* read. The term *acquired dyslexia* refers to disorders of reading which occur as a result of brain damage: a person who was previously literate now has impaired reading ability.

Those with *surface dyslexia* can no longer use the direct route and visually recognize words with which they were familiar before their injury. Instead, they have to rely on the indirect route, which leads to problems with irregular words such as 'scythe' or 'listen'. Those with *phonological dyslexia*, on the other hand, cannot employ the indirect route and therefore cannot sound-out words but they can still utilize the direct route.

As written text typically consists of sentences it must be parsed, or analysed for syntactic structure, by breaking it down into its component parts. (As the same is true of speech, the following discussion also applies to speech perception.) The sentence 'The elephant stole an orange' can be parsed as demonstrated below.

Parsing 'The elephant stole an orange'

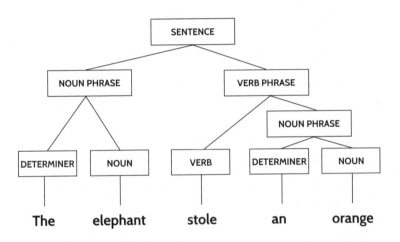

Although we are usually successful in parsing sentences, this is not inevitably the case. Sometimes, our *cognitive parser* slips up and produces an inaccurate analysis. This can be seen in what are called *garden-path sentences*. Look at this very well-known example:

The old man the boat.

How did you cope with this sentence? If you found it hard to interpret, do not worry. It is hard to decipher as it 'leads us down the garden path'. This occurs because the cognitive parser analyses the sentence in a particular way, and later information reveals that this analysis is incorrect. Consequently, the cognitive parser must return to the sentence to analyse it correctly.

In 'The old man the boat', the first three words group together to offer a meaning that the sentence is going to concern an elderly man. That is, 'old' is taken to be an adjective describing the noun 'man'. The remainder of the sentence, however, makes it clear that this cannot be the case. In correcting the analysis, the cognitive parser has to determine that it is 'the old' which group – 'old' now being a noun – and that 'man' is a verb, as in handling or staffing the boat.

How sentences are parsed has been accounted for in different ways and we shall be looking at the *garden-path, constraint-based* and *unrestricted race* approaches.

Garden-path theory takes its name from the way in which, when parsing, we can be misled by garden-path sentences. The theory possesses two stages: firstly, a sentence's grammatical structure alone is determined; if this interpretation proves to be mistaken based on other non-syntactic sources of information, then another analysis occurs.

Lyn Frazier was the first person to forward the garden-path model and the version to be discussed below is the one she developed with Keith Rayner. They explored how garden-path sentences are parsed by recording the eye movements of their participants as they read. They concluded that syntactic ambiguity is resolved by the cognitive parser using *minimal attachment* and *late closure*. Minimal attachment involves constructing the simplest syntactic structure, but this must be consistent with the rules of well-formed language. Late closure refers to new information being attached to the clause or phrase currently being processed – so long as the grammatical rules of the language allow for this. If minimal attachment and late closure are not in agreement, the issue between them is settled by pursuing the former. If further information reveals that the syntactic structure which has been constructed is incorrect, another analysis is pursued.

Constraint-based models have a contrasting perspective on parsing. They propose that syntax is only one of many interacting factors constraining sentence interpretation. While syntax is of course important, it is no more important for sentence interpretation than, for instance, semantic, contextual or plausibility information. Consequently, when dealing with an ambiguous syntactic structure, the constraint-based approach proposes that all factors that constrain the structure's interpretation are taken into account and they activate different possible analyses. These analyses then compete with each other until one is more successful than the others.

To give the reader a better idea of constraining factors, let's begin with context. With the previous example, 'The old man the boat', this is presented as a stand-alone sentence without any context. When context is included, it becomes easier to interpret, as in: 'For some time now there has been a lack of young sailors. The old man the boat'. Additionally, as highlighted above, 'man' can be used as a noun and a verb. This applies to other words too, such as 'rose' (the flower versus getting to one's feet), while some words may possess several interpretations. 'Port', for example, can be used as a noun in a number of ways: it might refer to a shipping port such as Liverpool; a socket on a computer; the alcoholic drink; or the left side of a ship or aircraft. In cases such as these, frequency can play a role as one reading of the word can be more frequent than another. Another constraining factor in association with verbs is that they are not all identical in terms of the structure which accompanies them. For instance, while 'The elephant awoke' is a structure which is complete by itself, 'the elephant stole' is incomplete. 'Stole' not only requires a stealer – in this case the elephant – but also whatever it was that was stolen. Finally, a rearrangement of the sentence to 'The orange stole an elephant', shows that meaning, or semantics, constrain interpretation given that the designated stealer must be able to actively steal. World knowledge also informs us that the sentence is implausible – an orange cannot steal an elephant!

Roger van Gompel and colleagues' unrestricted race model is both similar to, and different from, the garden-path and constraint-based models. As with the latter, this account proposes that resolving ambiguous syntactic structure is not limited to a particular kind of information, that is, it is 'unrestricted'. Furthermore, the number of different information sources available, accompanied by their strength, determine how quickly a structural analysis is put together. Since the ambiguity of a sentence means that more than one structure is possible, all potential structures are assembled and they compete with each other in terms of how quickly they are constructed. In other words, they 'race' against each other and the one that wins the race is the one which is selected. If, however, extra material reveals that this analysis is incorrect, then a second stage is necessitated and the sentence has to be analysed again.

Access to the meaning of text can be gained in similar ways as from the spoken word. Context, for example, sets up expectations for what is likely to appear in whatever is being read. If this is a report on a Premier League football match, soccer-related words would be anticipated and this expectation would allow for words such as 'goal', 'ball' and 'offside' to be read more swiftly. Inferences are also drawn from text to establish meaning. In the following

Margaret Rutherford, who appeared in Murder, She Said.

sentence, heat and temperature are made plain and meaning can be drawn explicitly from what is written: 'The day was starting to be hot; the mercury on the thermometer was already at 33°C'. In the next sentence, however, meaning can be acquired implicitly: 'The sun shone down and he removed his coat'. The two points are made close together and because the sun provides heat, it is reasonable to infer that the sun is responsible for the coat's removal.

The meaning of text is also acquired through the use of prosody, signalled via the use of punctuation. For example, the 1961 film title, *Murder, She Said,* has a comma to indicate a pause is required between the first and second words. This draws attention to 'murder' and helps with the lack of speech marks which would customarily indicate something has been said within text. Rhythm can be controlled too with semi-colons and colons, while full stops, or periods, indicate a longer pause is necessitated and that there is a break between ideas. Exclamation and question marks can give some indication of intonation because we know that a voice rises with a question, and when we call or shout out, as in 'Thank you!'

Indeed, the use of punctuation in writing can change the meaning of what is written quite considerably. Consider the following: 'In the library were the cricketers, Elizabeth Bennet and Charlotte Lucas'. The pause signalled by the comma indicates that the two people named are the cricketers. However, if one extra piece of punctuation is added, the meaning changes: 'In the library were the cricketers, Elizabeth Bennet, and Charlotte Lucas'. Compared with the initial statement, the addition of an Oxford comma after the first surname signals that the library holds at least four people (given that cricketers is plural); those who are cricketers plus Elizabeth Bennet and Charlotte Lucas.

However, despite punctuation being helpful in signalling prosody, it fails to match the prosody found in speech. Punctuation simply lacks the ability to capture the nuances of intonation, rhythm and pitch found in the spoken word.

Paul Broca and Carl Wernicke.

APHASIA: AN EXAMPLE OF LANGUAGE DISORDER

What follows is not a comprehensive discussion of the topic of *aphasia*. Instead, only four aphasias are considered; they are not discussed in their entirety, nor has any distinction been made between differences which may exist between individual people.

Aphasia is an acquired language disorder arising after a brain injury such as a stroke. It affects spoken and written communication. It is an acquired disorder because, prior to the brain injury which led to aphasia, the person had normal speech and language. The earliest descriptions of aphasia came from Paul Broca (1861) and Carl Wernicke (1874), but the disorders they reported were characterized differently. Consequently, *Broca's aphasia* (often called *expressive aphasia* or *non-fluent aphasia*) and *Wernicke's aphasia* (also known as *receptive aphasia* and *fluent aphasia*) are distinguished. In broad terms, the former is associated with language production problems whereas the latter is associated with an inability to comprehend spoken language. Although the two aphasias occur separately, it is also possible for them to appear together.

The speech of someone with Broca's aphasia lacks fluency. Its characteristics include: difficulty in starting to speak and the effortful articulation of what is spoken; transposed phonemes; problems in finding the right word; shorter utterances than is typical of spoken language; and telegraphic speech. To give an idea of what might happen, suppose the person wishes to say 'Salma is feeding the cat'; this might be expressed as 'Sal… Salma… f…f… feed… cat'. Note that although what is said has fewer words, those words are nevertheless correct and they communicate a message.

Producing writing may present particular difficulties for those people who are right-handed. Putting this simply, in the majority of people, especially those who are right-handed, the left half of the brain – the left hemisphere – is responsible for language. Language production is linked to the frontal lobe of the left hemisphere. It is also the case that the left half of the brain's frontal lobe controls muscle movement on the right side of the body. Now, when endeavouring to write, we must produce accurate language and, typically, employ our dominant hand while writing. This means that if a right-handed person has damage to the left half of the brain such that language production and right-sided muscle movement are both affected, they are now presented with two problems. Firstly, in order to write something, all that is required for language production will be needed and, secondly, this has to be physically produced. In handwriting, for example, each individual letter has to be formed and it is necessary to move from one letter to the next and, likewise, from one word to the next. When the right hand cannot complete the requisite actions, the person may use their left hand. However, the difficulties associated with producing language coupled with being unpractised at writing with the non-dominant hand often leads to notably impaired results.

If a person has *pure* Broca's aphasia, that is they have language production problems alone, then comprehension will be intact. If the Broca's aphasia is not pure, however, although comprehension is relatively intact certain problems nevertheless exist. For example, difficulties can appear when speech has complicated syntax and grammar; additionally, when reading, the individual may read nouns and verbs but then guess at what a sentence means. Suppose the sentence to be read is 'The cat that Salma is feeding is purring'. If the reader is able to understand 'Salma', 'cat', 'feeding' and 'purring', guesswork will likely lead to the sentence being comprehended correctly. It is highly unlikely that Salma would purr and impossible that the cat would be feeding Salma! On the other hand, 'The cyclist that the man passed shouted' necessitates that a reader can use its syntax. Understanding 'cyclist', 'man', 'passed' and 'shouted' by themselves does not let the reader know who was doing the passing nor who was doing the shouting.

Wernicke's aphasia is different from Broca's aphasia in that speech does not possess effortful articulation and it is fluent, with prosody. However, it is possible for grammar to be affected with

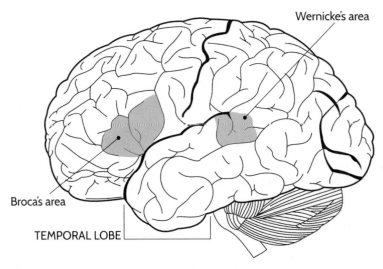

The position of Broca's Area and Wernicke's Area in the left hemisphere (half) of the brain.

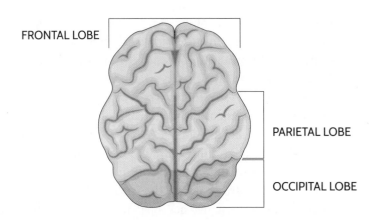

Broca and Wernicke identified different patterns of language impairment associated them with particular areas of the brain. These regions are now known as Broca's Area (in the frontal lobe) and Wernicke's Area (in the temporal lobe). Modern research has shown that the location of language functions in the brain is complex: for example, Broca's aphasia arises with damages to parts of the brain beyond Broca's Area.

function words (for example, 'the', 'that') being included incorrectly and syntactic word order may not be upheld (*paragrammatism*). Whereas Broca's aphasia is associated with short utterances, the speech of someone with Wernicke's aphasia is different in this regard. Utterances may be of a length that matches typical, conversational speech, or they may be significantly longer. One of the reasons for this is *circumlocution*. A person with Wernicke's aphasia uses fewer content words, such as nouns and verbs and missing words can be compensated for through the use of paraphrases. Since paraphrases inevitably consist of more words, speech thus becomes longer. For the listener, lengthy speech can be hard to follow and is made more difficult to understand due to the presence of semantic, phonemic and neologistic paraphasias.

A *paraphasia* is an error in speech production. Semantic errors involve producing a word related in meaning to the intended word (for example, 'car' is said rather than 'lorry'; 'pear' instead of 'orange'), or they may involve substituting general words like 'thing' or 'stuff' in place of a more precise word. With phonemic paraphasia, phonemes do not appear appropriately (for example, 'braker' instead of 'baker'; 'bable' for 'table'). If this occurs several times within a word it results in a neologism, or a wholly new word. The *neologism* can be so markedly different from the intended word that it is unrecognizable as the original.

Speech comprehension is impaired in Wernicke's aphasia and a person's ability to read tends to be similar to how well they understand speech. Additionally, although an individual may be able to produce writing in terms of forming letters and putting these together to create words, the writing's content is impaired in that what is written matches the person's speech output.

A third type of aphasia that has been identified is called *conduction aphasia*. Its defining characteristic is that a person exhibits difficulty in repeating what has been said to them. Although this feature is also found in both Broca's and Wernicke's aphasias, conduction aphasia is different from these aphasias too, as well as being similar to them in other ways. It is associated with:

fluent speech accompanied by phonemic paraphasias (similar to Wernicke's aphasia but unlike Broca's); relatively good speech comprehension (unlike Wernicke's aphasia and more like Broca's); and, as with Broca's but unlike Wernicke's aphasia, someone with conduction aphasia is aware of their speech production errors. Indeed, a person with conduction aphasia may repeatedly try to correct their errors, getting closer and closer to the desired word. With respect to the other elements of language, writing may be affected; problems arise with reading, if reading aloud, but what is read is comprehended.

As the name implies, *global aphasia* refers to a severe impairment of all language functions. Although this does not mean that a person has no language whatsoever, communication is very limited. Speech, for example, may consist of single words, repeated syllables, overlearned material, such as saying stock words or phrases, or being able to repeat the days of the week. Speech comprehension, reading and writing are all impaired. As language ability is so profoundly compromised, someone with global aphasia may resort to using non-linguistic means of communication and watch out for non-linguistic cues in order to comprehend the person who is speaking to them.

Key Points

- Language comprises words and rules; words comprise phonemes; phonemes combine to make morphemes. Grammar consists of syntax and semantics and involves the rules of using words meaningfully. Semantics put meaning to morphemes; syntax comprises the rules of forming and structuring language.
- Speech production begins with meaning; we plan in clauses; syntax is determined; morphemes are converted to phonemes; phonemes are articulated with the inclusion of prosody.
- Evidence for planning in clauses comes from pauses and speech errors, such as when inflections are added.
- Common ground, or shared knowledge, facilitates spoken communication.
- Theories of speech production include Dell's interactive spreading activation model and WEAVER++.
- Speech perception requires phoneme detection; this is made harder by speech being different from person to person.
- Speech perception is assisted by: co-articulation; knowledge of a language; visual information; prosody; context and inferences.
- The cohort model accounts for word recognition in speech.
- Spoken and written sentences are parsed for their structure; models of parsing include the garden-path, constraint-based and unrestricted race approaches.

- Writing requires establishing the meaning to be conveyed; planning; generating phrases, clauses and sentences; creating words on a page or screen.
- Writing and speaking are different in that the former has more planning opportunities; delayed or no feedback; has more revisions; greater formality and longer, more complex sentences and vocabulary.
- Models of writing have been provided by Flower and Hayes, and Hayes.
- Eye movement in reading involves saccades, regressions and fixations; information is taken in during fixations.
- McClelland and Rumelhart proposed a model of how four-letter words are recognized; the Dual Route Cascaded model accounts for the pronunciation of a printed word.
- The meaning of text is gained through context, inferences and prosody signalled by punctuation.
- Aphasia is an acquired language disorder. The different types of aphasia include: Broca's aphasia, Wernicke's aphasia, conduction aphasia and global aphasia.

Chapter 6

Thinking

Let's begin with a question: *how would you define thinking?*

To date, your life will have been full of times when you were thinking about something, even if only considering whether to have a cup of coffee now, or later. Having to respond to the question required that you think. Perhaps you resolved that thinking concerns applying your mind to an issue; or else that it concerns forming an idea about something? You may also have replied that thinking is something that we do when we solve a problem, reason, or make a decision?

Now, some more questions:
1) *How good are you at problem solving?*
2) *How good are you at reasoning?*
3) *How good are you at decision making?*

Our effectiveness at problem solving, reasoning and decision making have been explored by psychologists and these three topics will be discussed in this chapter. First, however, let's be clear about what is meant by each.

When we problem solve, we must determine what should be done in order to arrive at a solution. Decision making involves having alternatives from which to choose, and doing so after their respective merits and disadvantages have been considered.

Rodin's Thinker.

Reasoning is based on formal logic; information is provided and based upon this evidence an assessment is made as to whether a specific conclusion may be drawn.

PROBLEM SOLVING

A problem has three elements. Initially, we begin with information or circumstances that create a situation which needs to be resolved. Secondly, a resolution to the situation must be achieved but, thirdly, there are challenges which must be overcome in order to arrive at the resolution. Moreover, it is not immediately apparent what should be done to achieve that resolution. However, some problems are more straightforward than others. Working through a mathematics question, for example, is a more precise and clear-cut problem than say, working out which one of you will be able to go shopping while taking into account work, childcare and responsibilities for older relatives. Since the latter kind of problem is more opaque, psychologists have typically focused on those problems which are better delineated.

Have you ever struggled to solve a problem and then suddenly the solution comes to mind? If so, you have had an *aha moment* and experienced insight. If you have also had the opportunity to consider how you arrived at that point, you will probably have noticed that you had been looking at the problem from different angles. Doing so involved a reorganization of the different parts of the problem to produce the aha moment; in other words, you engaged in what the Gestalt psychologists called *productive thinking*. Of course, not all problems are solved in this manner. You may well be able to think of occasions when you have methodically worked through a problem, drawing on your memory and past experiences, or techniques that have worked in the past. When you solved a problem in this manner, you engaged in what the Gestalt psychologists called *reproductive* thinking.

If you are asking yourself whether you would really have much awareness of how you are faring when completing a problem-solving task, the answer is yes. Janet Metcalfe and David Wiebe investigated performance on insight problems, along with non-insight and algebra problems, using feelings of 'warmth'. That is, the closer a person felt they were to the solution to a problem, the 'warmer' they felt; the further away they felt themselves to be the 'colder' they felt. It was discovered that algebra and non-insight problems exhibited a gradual increase in warmth over the course of problem solving, whereas insight problems were associated with a sudden increase in warmth.

Whether we engage in productive or reproductive thinking has consequences for problem solving. The Gestaltist, Max Wertheimer, highlighted the difference between productive and reproductive thinking in terms of teaching students how to calculate the area of a parallelogram (see A in the figure opposite). One technique involved thinking about the geometry of the parallelogram. Looking at the figure provided, a triangle exists to the left, at the end of the shape (see B), which can be flipped and moved to the right end of the shape (C), to create a new, rectangle shape. Now the area of the parallelogram can be calculated by working out the area of the rectangle. The alternative technique is to go through a stage-by-stage process involving a formula. Wertheimer found that although either method allowed for calculating the shape's area, the different techniques led to different transferable skills. The one which focused on the shape's geometry helped students to transfer what they learned to new, shape-related problems that they had not encountered previously. They could use productive thinking and consider new problems in terms of restructuring them. However, those who had learned the stage-by-stage technique did not have reproductive skills to transfer because they had not been provided with a formula that would apply to the new shapes.

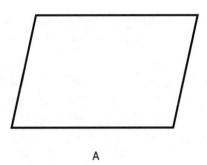

A

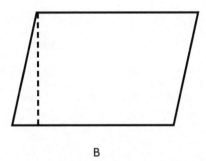

B

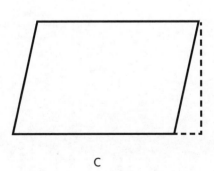

C

Max Wertheimer.

Evidently, if you are trying to solve a problem and drawing on previous experience is not working, it is worthwhile considering whether to engage in productive thinking and a restructure of the problem at hand.

Insight has been associated with both scientific and artistic advances and it is linked to particular kinds of benefits. For example, Peter Liljehadl reported that mathematics students who had gained insight felt less anxious about the subject and were prepared to pursue problem solving until the solution had been found. Additionally, Jasmin Kizilirmak and colleagues reported that insight led to deeper encoding and better memory for solutions to word problems.

Insight may be prompted if clues to a problem are present. This can be seen in a classic study by N.R.F. Maier. Participants entered a room where two pieces of string hung from the ceiling and the participants' task was to tie them together. However, this was a challenge, as the strings were positioned such that if a person went to one, got hold of it and then proceeded to try to get hold of the second string, they could not do so: the second string was out of reach. In addition to the strings, other items were also present in the room, including a pair of pliers. Based on the information you have so far, how would you attempt to resolve the problem?

The insight necessitated realizing that if the pliers were attached to one of the pieces of string, this piece could now be swung like a pendulum (see illustration overleaf). Once the string and pliers were swung, they would ultimately come sufficiently close to be caught, even when the participant was standing, holding the second piece of string. Now the two string lengths could be tied together. Clues that assisted the participants in solving the problem included brushing past a string, so that it moved. If this did not prompt the solution, a participant was offered the pliers and provided with the information that the tool could help the participant solve the problem.

Interestingly, when people went on to solve the problem subsequent to the string being moved, they were often unaware of what had prompted the solution. Additionally, being specifically supplied with the pliers did not guarantee a solution to the problem. The pliers had to be seen as a potential pendulum weight; if this could not be worked out by the participant and the tool was seen solely in terms of being something employed for taking a firm grip on objects, the problem was not resolved.

That certain participants could only see the pliers as a tool has probably hinted to you that past experience can hinder problem solving. It does this in different ways, such as our persisting with a *problem-solving set* and exhibiting *functional fixedness*.

A *mental set* exists when a technique that has previously been successful for problem solving is now applied to another problem, despite an easier alternative being available. This was shown by Abraham Luchins in his classic paper-based water jar problem. In this study, there were a series of problems involving three water jars, A, B and C. For each problem, the quantity of water contained within A, B and C was specified and there was also an amount of water which had to be achieved. The latter had to be arrived at by adding or subtracting the quantities of water specified under A, B and C. For example:

$A = 15$;　　$B = 39$;　　$C = 3$.　　Target amount $= 18$

There are two ways in which this problem can be solved; one technique consists of employing a long formula, while the other comprises a shorter, easier way. The long solution is to proceed with the following:

1. Fill jar B to its size of 39.
2. Now fill jar A from B, $(39^{\text{Jar B}} - 15^{\text{Jar A}} = 24^{\text{Jar B}})$.
3. Fill C from B's 24, $(24^{\text{Jar B}} - 3^{\text{Jar C}} = 21^{\text{Jar B}})$.
4. Fill C again from B's 21, $(21^{\text{Jar B}} - 3^{\text{Jar C}} = 18^{\text{Target}})$.

The shorter, easier way is as follows: fill Jar A and fill Jar C, $(15^{\text{Jar A}} + 3^{\text{Jar C}})$.

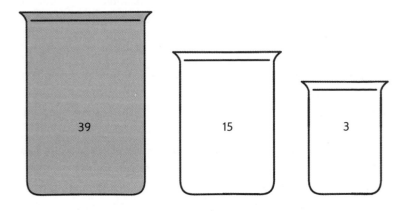

Water jar problem.

Luchins found that if participants had solved problems that necessitated using the formula: Jar B – Jar A – 2 Jar C, they typically continued to use this solution on problems which could be solved more easily. That is, they pursued the resolution pattern they had established – their mental set – even though an alternative was available. Other participants who attempted only those problems which could be resolved by a shorter route (either Jar A + Jar C or Jar A – Jar C), typically discovered and employed this solution.

As indicated above, Luchins' task was paper-based, therefore the question arises as to whether a mental set is inevitable, or whether it is affected by how a problem is addressed. This was examined by Frédéric Vallée-Tourangeau and colleagues in two experiments. In one, participants followed the original, paper-based procedure. This is noninteractive and it requires participants to mentally conceive the physical jars, water and the act of pouring. In the other experiment, participants completed their task in an interactive, practical way, with physical water and jars at a sink. Again, participants were given problems which necessitated all three jars and then they switched to a key problem which could be resolved by an easier answer. This comparison showed that those in the interactive experiment, with the practical items, had greater success than those working only in paper format. As Vallée-Tourangeau and his co-researchers have pointed out, dealing with real water jars and water allowed for solutions to be discovered that were not simulated mentally. Thus, the mental set of Luchins' work may have developed because all aspects of what participants had to complete were very similar. In contrast, in the practical version, greater success occurred because everything with which the participants were dealing was not so very similar due to its dynamic nature.

Functional fixedness arises when we think about objects in terms of their possessing fixed or stable functions, such that we cannot appreciate how an object may be used to solve a problem outside its usual function. This can be seen in Karl Duncker's box/candle problem. Imagine that you have been given a box of matches, a box containing some drawing pins, and a third box with some small candles. Your task is to fix the candles to the wall, so that each one acts properly as a light – but you may only use the supplies provided. How would you solve this problem?

The solution is as follows:
1. Empty out the boxes.
2. Tack the empty boxes to the wall using the drawing pins.
3. Fix a candle to each of the boxes. That is, use a match to light the candle; after some wax has melted, pour this into the box and you can now fix the candle to the box in the melted wax.

In Duncker's study, participants were either given their items in boxes, or they received their items already removed from the boxes. Those in the former group were markedly less successful in finding the solution than those supplied with their items separate from the boxes. This was because presenting the items within the boxes fixed the function of the boxes as containers, so that reconceptualizing the boxes as potential candle holders became less likely.

Candle, drawing pin and match.

Let's shift our attention now to another important issue in problem solving – the ways in which we attempt to solve problems. One option is to apply an *algorithm* which necessitates pursuing a series of stages to solve a problem. This technique will definitely lead to solving the problem, but its accompanying disadvantage is that an algorithm can be complicated and time-consuming. As highlighted by Allen Newell and Herb Simon's work on problem solving (mentioned in the Introduction), we can also problem solve by adopting heuristics. A *heuristic* is a 'rule of thumb', or a general rule which often provides a correct answer.

The *means-ends heuristic* involves asking yourself what you want to achieve – your 'ends'. You also ask yourself what is preventing you from achieving your goal and what can get you from your current state to your goal/ends – this is your 'means'. The move from your current situation to achieving your goal requires establishing sub-goals, or smaller goals. As you work through each sub-goal, you progress to your overall 'ends'. An informal example of this can be seen in Tariq's problem.

TARIQ'S PROBLEM

Tariq has hired a van and, at one point in his journey, very bad parking means he has no alternative but to manoeuvre the van over a grass verge in order to get on with his journey. Unfortunately, though, the ground is soft due to rain and one of the van's wheels spins and the vehicle will not move. Tariq has nothing to put under the tyre of the wheel so that it will grip. He looks around and notices that there is a joinery business nearby. He goes to get a piece of off-cut wood; he puts this under the tyre for grip and the van moves.

Tariq's problem-solving using means-ends analysis can be described in the following way:

Goal? – To get the van moving.

What is preventing this? – Soft ground.

What will let me achieve my goal? – Solid surface.

Sub-goals? – Identify suitable solid surfaces/objects on which tyre will grip. Find suitable object.

A more formal example of the means-ends heuristic in action can be seen in John C. Thomas's Hobbits and Orcs problem. Before proceeding further, it should be explained that Hobbits and Orcs are creatures from J.R.R. Tolkien's Middle Earth fantasy novels. Orcs are aggressive and large, whereas Hobbits are much smaller and non-aggressive, though they can be very courageous if circumstances necessitate this. In the problem, there are three of each creature and all must cross a river using a boat which will only hold one-to-two of them at a time. The boat always has to have at least one Hobbit or one Orc every time it crosses the river and the Hobbits can never be outnumbered by the Orcs on either side of the river.

Like Tariq, people presented with this problem recognize their end goal (that is, all Hobbits and Orcs transferred to the other side of the river), and that sub-goals will be required to be successful. Yet, while Tariq found a solution that worked using means-end analysis, this is not always the case with those endeavouring to solve the current problem. The difficulty lies in the necessity of returning a Hobbit and an Orc to the original side of the river. People do not often spot this requirement, and even if they do, they can be reticent in returning two creatures to where they started from. This is because returning individuals to the original river bank means departing from the final goal.

Another problem-solving approach is the *hill climbing heuristic*. This way of finding a solution follows a strategy in which, at every point of the problem-solving process, there is always a move toward what the problem solver wants to achieve. Imagine that you have decided to climb a hill in England's Lake District. As you pursue your route to the summit, there will be points along the way where you have to choose which way to go. Using the hill-climbing heuristic, you will always opt to move upwards; you will select the way that, in the short term, will take you higher. Yet, the attendant disadvantage with this approach is that it will not get you to the summit. Sometimes, when hill-climbing, it is necessary

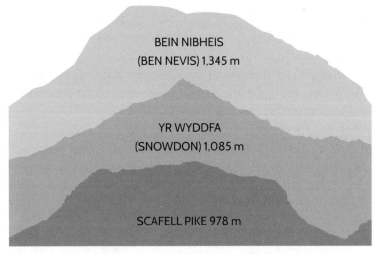

BEIN NIBHEIS
(BEN NEVIS) 1,345 m

YR WYDDFA
(SNOWDON) 1,085 m

SCAFELL PIKE 978 m

The highest mountains found in Scotland, Wales and England. When people apply the hill-climbing heuristic, they attempt to solve a problem by always moving towards their end goal.

to descend before reascending, or to go around an obstacle before reascending. Constantly moving upwards may take you elsewhere than the summit. Applying this to other types of problem, *always* following short-term options that appear to lead to the end goal will not necessarily get you to that point.

Another way to problem-solve is to do so by *analogy*. This involves examining the current problem and recognizing that it is similar to a previous problem that was solved. The solution to the earlier problem can now be employed to resolve the current issue. Of course, in order for this way of problem solving to be successful, it is essential that there is a similar problem available upon which to draw, that the person must be able to recognize the similarities between the two problems, and that the information relating to the similar problem can be accessed correctly.

REASONING

As mentioned earlier, reasoning is based on formal logic. Although most people are not trained in formal logic, it is nevertheless still worth asking whether they can reason in a logical fashion.

One way of exploring this has been to examine people's success or otherwise with *conditional* or *propositional* reasoning. This is based in *propositional calculus,* which uses logical operators such as *if* and *not*. A reasoning task consists of three parts. The first part comprises two propositions; the first, or antecedent proposition begins *if...*, while the second, or *consequent proposition* begins, *then...*, as in:

If the candle is lit, then the room will be bright.

In the second part of the task, an extra piece of information either *affirms* or *denies* one of the previous propositions. That is, it states whether one of the propositions is true or false. Thus, for the example above, this would be one of:

The candle is lit;   The candle is not lit;
The room is bright;   the room is not bright.

In the third part of the reasoning task, a conclusion is provided which is either correct, or *valid,* or, it is incorrect, or *invalid.* This means we could have:

> *If the candle is lit, then the room will be bright.*
> *The candle is lit.* (This affirms the antecedent proposition.)
> *Therefore, the room is bright.* (This is the conclusion.)

Given that the antecedent and consequent propositions can be both affirmed or denied, there are consequently four patterns altogether; two of which lead to valid conclusions and two of which lead to invalid conclusions, according to propositional calculus. These are outlined below.

(i) Affirmation of the Antecedent	(ii) Denial of the Antecedent
If the candle is lit, then the room will be bright.	If the candle is lit, then the room will be bright.
The candle is lit.	The candle is not lit.
Therefore, the room is bright.	Therefore, the room is not bright.
VALID	INVALID

(iii) Affirmation of the Consequent	(iv) Denial of the Consequent
If the candle is lit, then the room will be bright.	If the candle is lit, then the room will be bright.
The room is bright.	The room is not bright.
Therefore, the candle is lit.	Therefore, the candle is not lit.
INVALID	VALID

Affirmation of the antecedent (i), is called *modus ponens* and denial of the consequent (iv), *modus tollens*. When considering propositional reasoning tasks, people are typically more successful with the former compared with the latter.

With reasoning tasks like those in (ii) – denial of the antecedent, and (iii) – affirmation of the consequent – it is common for people to determine that the conclusions are valid rather than invalid. Yet, if we look at these more closely, we can see how the conclusions are invalid. With (ii) denial of the antecedent, the room may still be bright for other reasons, such as someone opened the curtains and sunshine is pouring through the window, or somebody switched on the electric light. With (iii) affirmation of the consequent, the candle does not have to be lit for the room to be bright: curtains may be open or an electric light switched on.

People make errors with denial of the antecedent and affirmation of the consequent because they do not reason according to formal logic. Formal logic requires that a conclusion is *always* the case but people do not follow this regulation and they also rely on world knowledge. Reliance on world knowledge can be seen in the following example:

If I use a hammer, then I will hit my thumb.
I use a hammer.
Therefore, I will hit my thumb.

As you can see, this is another instance of affirmation of the antecedent and, therefore, following the principles of logic, the conclusion is valid. Unsurprisingly, though, this conclusion appears invalid according to everyday experience. Using a hammer does not inevitably lead to hitting one's thumb and it is more unlikely than likely that this will happen if the person using the hammer is proficient with the tool.

Another deductive reasoning task is the *Wason Selection Task,* devised by Peter Wason. The standard version of the Wason Selection Task has four cards, each of which has a number on one side and a letter on the other. Two cards are presented with the letter uppermost and two are presented with the numbers uppermost. The image below is an example of how this could look.

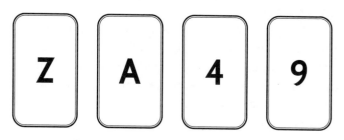

A rule is supplied in conjunction with the cards:

If the card has a Z on one side, then there is a 4 on the other side of the card.

The task is to determine which card, or cards, would have to be turned over, to discover whether the rule is true or false. Have a go at the task. Which card, or cards, would you pick to determine whether the rule is true or false?

Typically, participants who complete this kind of exercise select the Z card, or they opt for the Z and 4 cards. That is, they seek to confirm that the rule is true. The cards which should be turned over are those with Z and 9. This is because if Z is inspected and it does not have a 4 on its reverse, the rule is evidently false.

Similarly, if card 9 is turned and there is a Z, the rule is again clearly false. If 4 is chosen, the information it provides will not be helpful in deciding the accuracy, or otherwise, of the rule. If the 4 has a Z on the reverse, we cannot say definitively that the rule is true: it may be, but equally, it may not be. In other words, to determine the rule's validity, it is necessary to look for whether the rule can be falsified, or disproved. Yet people are reluctant to adopt this approach.

Of course, it is possible to argue that cards with letters and numbers leads to an abstract task, unlike the kinds of reasoning we might encounter day to day. Consequently, other selection studies have been conducted which have greater ecological validity; that is, they have a greater relationship to everyday life. Two of these are considered below.

Wason and Diana Shapiro produced a more realistic study by linking travel destinations to modes of transport. Of the four cards used, two showed the names of northern English cities – Manchester and Leeds – and the other two means of transport – car and train. The rule involved always travelling to Manchester by car. In this case, to determine whether the rule is true, the Manchester and train cards need to be inspected. This is because turning the Manchester card reveals if an arrival has ever been other than by car, and turning the train card shows whether a train has been used for going to Manchester. Compared with using a letter and number form of the Wason Selection Task, the researchers found that this format led to greater success.

In the study by Richard Griggs and James Cox, two selection tasks were used. One was abstract, akin to the Wason investigation discussed above, while the second one was more realistic. The realistic task again involved four cards which read: beer, coke, 16, 22. One side of each card stated a person's age and the other side what they were drinking. The rule was that to drink beer a person must be aged over 19. No one got the abstract problem correct but more than 70 per cent of those completing the drink/age problem selected the correct card (16).

Together, the studies reveal that, when reasoning, we are more successful if we can draw on experience rather than having to rely on abstract, formal logic. Other studies have shown that even non-specific knowledge can help. This said, in daily life, we probably will not have time nor the inclination to go through all options which refute whether something is the case or not: we will opt for what appears to be most practical.

Syllogisms have also been used to examine how people reason. A *categorical syllogism* consists of two premises and a conclusion, and the task is to determine if the conclusion is true or false from the premises. The premises and conclusion belong to one of four different kinds of descriptions which characterize the relationship between two categories:

(i) All A are B
(universal affirmative)

(iii) Some A are B
(particular affirmative)

(ii) No A are B
(universal negative)

(iv) Some A are not B
(particular negative)

Examples of categorical syllogisms include:
All people are human   *Some Star Trek fans are scientists*
All archivists are people   *Some scientists are cyclists*
Therefore, all archivists are human   *Therefore, some Star Trek*
                                                   fans are cyclists.

Whether the conclusion can be deduced from the premises depends entirely upon the rules of logic, irrespective of whether we agree or disagree with what is stated, and conclusions may be valid, invalid, or it may be impossible to decide either way. In the examples above, the first syllogism is valid but the second one cannot be determined. Although the Star Trek syllogism may seem to be valid because it is likely that some people who are fans of the various series and films also cycle, following logic, the conclusion does not automatically follow from the premises. This is because, logically, there are two possibilities: *no Star Trek fans are cyclists* and *all Star Trek fans are cyclists.*

Unsurprisingly, people often find it challenging when faced with syllogisms. Part of the challenge is appreciating that the language of syllogistic reasoning does not follow the same kinds of rules that we use when communicating. Take the word 'some'; to how many do you consider this word refers? In syllogistic reasoning, 'some' means at least one and possibly all. Furthermore, 'All A are B' does not also mean 'All B are A' – though they may be. Even though explanations of the rules of logic can help people complete categorical reasoning tasks more successfully, knowledge and beliefs often override the application of logic's rules and lead to logically inaccurate conclusions.

DECISION MAKING

Decision making involves choosing from the available options. Much work in this field has been completed by Amos Tversky and Daniel Kahneman who have shown that we often use rules of thumb, or heuristics, to help us make decisions. However, in doing so we are often led astray.

One heuristic that we employ is the *representativeness heuristic,* which is a shortcut for assessing how likely something is; whether whatever we are dealing with is representative, or typical of the group to which it belongs. The use of this heuristic was found by Tversky and Kahneman when they presented participants with different kinds of problems. One of these related to tossing a coin six times and participants were asked to indicate which sequence of heads (H) and tails (T) was the most likely to occur:

(i) HHHTTT;   (ii) HTHTHT;   (iii) HTTHTH.

What do you think?

Sequence (iii) is often selected as the most likely. However, following the *Theory of Probability* (a mathematical theory as to how likely it is that an event will occur), all three sequences are equally likely to arise. Option (iii) is chosen more often because it looks as though it is more random – as a rule of thumb, its sequence appears more random.

Tossing a coin. If the coin is unbiased (i.e. it is not fixed to come down on one side rather than the other), the chance of it landing as a head or a tail is 50:50.

Other errors are made when using the representativeness heuristic. For example, people often assume that a small sample represents the population from which it is drawn. However, this is not the case: such a sample often gives a false indication of the true nature of the population and it is large samples which better represent their parent populations. Additionally, people often ignore base-rate information. Kahneman and Tversky showed their participants personality descriptions supposedly drawn at random from a group of 100 professionals, all of whom were either lawyers or engineers. Half of the participants were told the group of 100 consisted of 70 lawyers and 30 engineers; the other half were informed that the group comprised 30 lawyers and 70 engineers. The participants' task was to assess whether the personality description belonged to a lawyer or an engineer. Irrespective of which 70 and 30 information was supplied, participants typically decided that it was more probable that the individual described was an engineer because he sounded more stereotypically like an engineer. Yet, whether he was more likely to be a lawyer or an engineer would be affected by the number of occupational descriptions of each within the pool of 100.

A further error in relation to the representativeness heuristic comes from the *conjunction fallacy*. Kahneman and Tversky provided participants with a description of a woman called Linda. This characterized her as 31, single, clever and outspoken. During her student years, Linda had deep concerns regarding social justice and discrimination and she participated in anti-nuclear demonstrations. After the description, participants were asked to consider the likelihood of Linda being: (a) a bank teller or (b) a bank teller active in the feminist movement. Although the depiction of the study provided here is a paraphrase, take another look at Linda's description – which option would you select as the most likely?

In the study, most people selected the second option which characterized Linda as a bank teller plus being active in the feminist movement. It appeared more representative of what she would be like than bank teller alone, even though the question asked how *likely* she was to be one or the other. In fact (b) is not more likely than (a). According to the mathematical conjunction rule, the probability of two events occurring together cannot be greater than the probability of one event occurring by itself. Naturally, it is fair to argue that most people are not trained in the mathematical technicalities of the conjunction rule. However, it was also found that even those with advanced statistical knowledge still fell foul of the conjunction fallacy.

Another means of decision making is to use the *availability heuristic*. Tversky and Kahneman asked participants whether a word, randomly drawn from an English text, was more likely to (a) begin with a K, or, (b) have K as the third letter. Which do you think is the correct answer? If you opted for (a), this is what most people think, but (b) is the correct answer. The researchers argued that (a) is selected on the basis that it is easier to retrieve words beginning with K from long-term memory than to retrieve words where K is the third letter. Applying this more broadly, we make judgements about the frequency or probability of events dependent upon how many of those events we can remember.

Let's turn now to a different heuristic. The following questions are adaptations from work by Karen Jacowitz and Daniel Kahneman; you may have to guess with them but that is all right:

Map of Scotland.

(1) Is the population of Scotland over or under 300,000?

(2) What is the population of Scotland?

The next question assumes that you do not know the actual population of Scotland – do you think that your answer to (1) would affect your answer to (2)?

One way of making a decision about number is to start with an initial approximation – the anchor – and then adjust from this. However, the *anchoring and adjustment heuristic* causes a problem: the anchor that we use pulls the adjustment in its direction. Consequently, the chances are that you potentially under-estimated Scotland's population because the figure in (1) exerted a pulling effect in its direction. (Based on data from the Census, in 2023 Scotland's population was estimated to be 5.4 million.)

Here is another example, based on a study by Tversky and Kahneman, and you will need a friend for this. Please note, you are not being asked to perform a whole calculation! Instead, you should each take five seconds to estimate the answer to one of the questions below. Your friend should complete (a) and you (b).

(a) 1 x 2 x 3 x 4 x 5 x 6 x 7 x 8 x 9 x 10

(b) 10 x 9 x 8 x 7 x 6 x 5 x 4 x 3 x 2 x 1

Are your estimates the same? Mathematically, they should be identical, but who gave the lower estimate? Typically, it should be your friend.

When Tversky and Kahneman gave their two series of numbers to participants, they either ran 1...8 or 8...1. The product of each was 40,320; yet, although estimates were far too low for both orders, the median (see box overleaf) was substantially higher for the series 8-1, than 1-8. In other words, the anchors provided in the two series of numbers (1 versus 8) affected the estimated products and ensured that they were both too low.

If you are wondering about the product of (a) and (b) it is 3,628,800.

> **THE MEDIAN**
> The median is a measure of central tendency. That is, it is a description of the average value of scores.
>
> It is calculated by taking a set of scores and ordering them from lowest to highest. The score which falls in the middle is the median.

Finally, you may be asking why we even use heuristics if they lead us so badly astray? Quite simply, much of the time they make life easier. When dealing with information, we often have limited time and limited cognitive capacity to cope with everything and all possible options. What we should ensure, though, is that it is appropriate to use a given heuristic when it is employed.

Key Points

- Problem solving involves determining what must be done to achieve a solution. The solution is based on current circumstances and what challenges are in the way.
- Problem solving may be productive or reproductive; either can be successful, but reproductive thinking can lead to difficulty.
- Insight is associated with an 'aha' experience and can occur if provided with clues.
- Problem solving is impaired by mental set and functional fixedness.
- People may address problems by using algorithms, heuristics and analogy. Heuristics include the means-end and hill climbing heuristics; both can lead to errors.
- Reasoning is based on formal logic. It has been examined using propositional reasoning, the Wason Selection Task, and syllogisms. Errors are associated with each, but people are far more successful with realistic versions of Wason than abstract ones.
- Decision making involves selecting from alternatives and we use heuristics to do this because they make life easier when used appropriately.
- The representativeness heuristic may lead to error from making assumptions, ignoring base-rate information, and the conjunction fallacy.
- The availability heuristic leads to error based on the frequency of events recalled.
- The anchoring and adjustment heuristic pulls number estimates towards the anchor.

Chapter 7

Consciousness

The American psychologist William James (1840–1910) characterized consciousness as a river or stream, in which there is a
continuous flow of thoughts. A person's focus may be internal
(perceptions, thoughts, feelings) and it can be external (the
environment), but it is always a personal experience.

James's understanding of consciousness still has resonance
today, though our current understanding divides it as follows: (1)
as a state; (2) as experiences we can consciously access and report,
such as remembering something; (3) as one's own subjective,
private experience. Cognitive psychology focuses mostly upon
(2), but we will take a look at (1) and (3) as well, beginning with
consciousness as a state.

Although the state of consciousness is related to the state of
wakefulness, the two are not synonymous. Consciousness exists
as a continuum, with alert wakefulness at one end, through points
such as day-dreaming, sleep, and being anaesthetized, to lack of
consciousness and coma at the other end.

Currently, you are reading this book, so you must be in a state
of wakefulness. If it is assumed that you are also aware of your
external surroundings along with your perceptions, thoughts
and feelings, then your consciousness is high. If you were asleep,
though, you would lack wakefulness but be conscious. This
is demonstrated by it being possible to return you to a state of

William James.

wakefulness by speaking to you, or shaking you, for example. In contrast, someone who is in a coma cannot be similarly roused: a comatose state is associated with a lack of both wakefulness and conscious awareness.

When severe brain damage results in a vegetative state, the person exhibits wakefulness and typically, also a lack of consciousness. That is, the person will awake from sleep and there will be eye opening but the person does not engage meaningfully with their environment, nor is there any indication that the person has awareness of themself.

The word 'typically' is used because researchers have reported that a subgroup of those in a vegetative state have been found to show evidence of consciousness. For instance, Adrian Owen and colleagues reported findings concerning a 23-year-old woman who had been in a traffic accident which resulted in severe brain injury. Five months after the accident, she was diagnosed as being in a vegetative state. Using functional magnetic resonance imaging, the researchers compared the activity in the woman's brain with that of healthy volunteers. She was given verbal instructions which required her to mentally imagine: (a) playing a game of tennis and (b) visiting all the rooms in her house beginning at the front door. In both instances, the woman's brain activity was like that of the healthy volunteers. The researchers concluded from this that the woman retained conscious awareness: her brain activity revealed that she had done what was asked of her, which means she must have decided to follow the instructions. In other words, the woman was consciously aware of her environment and of herself.

If a severely brain damaged person can show signs of consciousness, it is reasonable to ask whether this conscious experience reflects that of someone who is healthy. Lorina Naci and colleagues obtained data from healthy participants which allowed them to establish the brain activity these people had in common, in response to watching an edited, eight-minute segment of an episode from the *Alfred Hitchcock Presents* TV series. The same film was also presented to two people with brain damage whose diagnosis had varied between a vegetative state and a minimally conscious state (that is, there is inconsistent but reproduced evidence of minimal awareness). The researchers argued that if consciousness was present, those with brain damage would have brain activity similar to the healthy participants. While one person did not show signs of consciousness, the second one did. Furthermore, that person appeared to have a conscious experience very similar to that of the healthy participants.

Before we move on to the other ways in which consciousness may be understood, look at the box below.

What follows is based on a real meeting and discussion.

It was spring and two people who had previously been neighbours met unexpectedly in the park. They both ordered coffee from the nearby café, went to sit on a bench and chatted, catching up with each other's news. After a while, Ayesha remarked on how lovely the park looked with the flowers and all the different shades of green. Alastair shook his head and said, 'I don't see what you see. I'm colour blind and it's shades of grey to me.'

How and why Ayesha could see green can be explained through the way in which visual perception operates, along with what goes on in the brain, and our nerve cells' means of communication. What Alastair could see can be explained in a similar fashion. However, these scientific descriptions of the means by which Ayesha and Alastair see, and what they see, will only go so far. When we experience a sensation, it is accompanied by a subjective feeling, such as Ayesha's feeling that the different shades of green were lovely. Yet, the origins of these private, personal experiences of 'greenness' or 'greyness' are a matter of debate.

Two friends on a park bench.

David Chalmers makes a distinction between what he refers to as the *easy problem* and the *hard problem* of consciousness. The easy problem involves explaining cognitive functions and linking them to the brain's physical processes. In terms of Ayesha and Alastair, this is the scientific description of what they see. The hard problem involves explaining how the brain's physical processes produce a subjective experience – the loveliness that Ayesha experienced looking at the flowers and the shades of green. Little is known about the answer to the hard problem, whereas much information has been gathered regarding the easy problem.

Another distinction has been made by Ned Block between *access consciousness* and *phenomenal consciousness*. Access consciousness is limited to what we are able to consciously report to ourselves and to others, while phenomenal consciousness is one's own subjective experience. Cognitive psychology typically focuses on the former but often uses the latter in terms of what participants report. For example, in memory research participants might be asked to indicate whether or not test stimuli have been encountered before. This kind of recognition task requires the personal experience of recognition to then be reported.

Cognitive psychology explores many conscious and unconscious processes and a few of these will now be considered, beginning with attention. Consciousness and attention are closely related but are not the same. While it is generally the case that we are consciously aware when focused attention is required, we are not necessarily conscious of those tasks which have become automatic. For example, somebody who is learning to drive must focus their attention on the task and this requires conscious awareness. An experienced driver, on the other hand, for whom driving has become an automatic process, may not be consciously aware that they have shifted the gearstick from second to third gear, say.

David Simons and Christopher Chabris have reported that most people believe that they would be aware of something unexpected in their visual field (see box on page 204) even if their attention were focused elsewhere. However, as the same researchers have demonstrated, we are not as consciously aware as we suppose. They had participants watch a 75-second film of a basketball match which involved six players, three on each team, who were differentiated by the colour of their shirts: black or white. To ensure that participants' attention was focused, their task was to count the number of occasions on which a ball was passed between players on each team. Beyond the halfway point of the film, a person dressed in a gorilla suit walked into the scene from left to right and was on screen for five seconds. The gorilla was noticed more often by those who were counting passes by the black-shirt team; half of those counting white-shirt team passes did not notice the gorilla. The researchers accounted for these results in terms of *inattentional blindness*. Those focused on black shirts had greater awareness of the gorilla because its colour was more like the shirts that were being attended. The participants who were focused on the white-shirt team, though, missed the gorilla due to inattentional blindness: focus on the white shirts meant that they failed to perceive the gorilla despite it being in plain sight.

In Simons' and Chabris' experiment, a person dressed in a gorilla suit walked into a basketball match, yet subjects asked to count passes between the players often failed to notice the gorilla.

VISUAL FIELD
To understand what is meant by 'visual field', read the
following in its entirety and then do what it describes.
   Look at the point directly ahead of you and concentrate
on that point. While you are doing this, you will be aware of
items to the left and right. The total area in which you can
see these items is your visual field.

As we saw in Chapter 4, memory research has revealed that
declarative and nondeclarative memories can be distinguished.
Declarative memory refers to those memories which we explicitly
or consciously remember, while nondeclarative memory
encompasses skills, abilities and other forms of learning which
are implicitly or unconsciously remembered. We know that these
kinds of memory are different from cases of amnesia, where
declarative memory is lost but nondeclarative memory remains.
Henry Molaison, for example, could not explicitly remember
where he lived but he could recall the skill of lawn-mowing and
he learned how to mirror draw.

   Another form of nondeclarative memory relates to *priming,*
in which current behaviour is affected by previous experience;
that is, if we are presented with a stimulus which is the same as
or related to a stimulus seen before, we are influenced in terms
of how we deal with the current item. A study exploring priming
effects might operate as follows: firstly, the participant is asked to
study a number of words, then after a delay they are given a word
stem completion task in which the initial letters of words are
provided followed by a blank. For instance, suppose that HOTEL
is one of the words among the group studied at the outset of the
investigation; at test, the letters HOT__ would be provided and
the participant would now have to complete the word. What is
of interest is whether the word so produced fits with what was
studied initially, or whether an unstudied option is selected.
If HOTEL is supplied as an answer, this is a primed response

whereas HOTLY would not be. If, overall, word completions generate more answers which fit with studied words compared with new words, then this produces evidence that a person has been affected by priming.

People with amnesia who have been tested in this way have been found to be affected by priming if, when completing the stem, they are asked to supply the first word that comes to mind. However, there is not an effect when asked to recall a word encountered previously based upon the letters supplied in the stem. To put this another way, priming occurs with nondeclarative memory but not with declarative memory, which requires a conscious recollection of what was studied beforehand.

Over time, considerable research has amassed regarding the brain areas which are involved in memory. The priming evidence from those with amnesia indicates that conscious recollection involves brain areas which are not depended upon for supplying the first word that comes to mind. Structures in the brain which have been associated with declarative memory include, for example, the hippocampus and the parahippocampal gyrus.

Memory research has also provided evidence that we are not necessarily capable of relating all of what we experience consciously. In Chapter 4, we looked at George Sperling's work on visual, sensory memory. He showed participants 12-letter arrays consisting of three rows of four letters which were presented for 1/20th of a second. Typically, participants reported four or five letters but said they had seen more: those items which could not be remembered were deemed to have faded away. However, when required to report only one line – which was not known in advance – participants' recall was good, whichever line's information had to be supplied, so long as a memory cue was provided close to seeing the original array. That participants were demonstrably aware of the presence of more letters than they could recount shows that their original conscious experience was richer than they could state. In turn, this means that a person's account of their conscious experience may well under-represent that experience.

Hippocampus

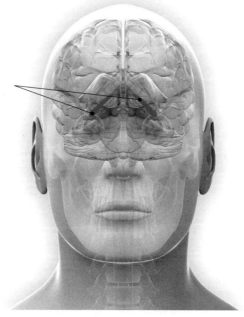

Hippocampus

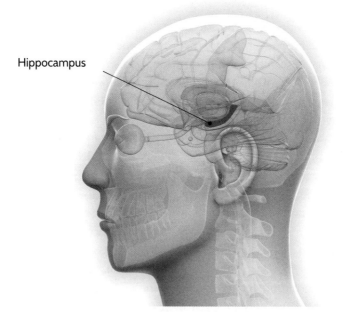

The hippocampus in the human brain. This structure is important in relation to declarative memory.

Consciousness has also been considered with reference to perception. *Blindsight* is a condition in which a person has damage to the primary visual cortex of the brain. As its name implies, this region of the brain is important for vision. In those with blindsight, individuals report that they cannot see in all or part of their visual field (see box on page 204). In other words, they subjectively report that they cannot see, or are blind in their visual field. However, when such a person is shown a stimulus in the blind region, such as a flash of light, they can nevertheless discriminate its location.

Data from those with blindsight has led to a number of interpretations of what the results mean. These include the conclusion that the ability to discriminate in the presence of blindness indicates consciousness is not required for such discrimination. Another analysis contends that for there to be visual awareness, or consciousness, visual information must be sent through the primary visual cortex. Furthermore, a question has been raised surrounding whether consciousness is actually useful to us, if visual tasks can be completed without its presence? In essence, all these interpretations concur that blindsight is indeed, 'blind' sight, and it is fair to say that this is the generally established position. There has, however, been dissent from this perspective: it has been argued, for example, that what has been accepted as blindness is instead degraded vision which simply cannot be subjectively reported. Of course, if this were to be demonstrated satisfactorily, then blindsight's current contribution to consciousness would have to be rethought.

Prosopagnosia resulting from brain damage leads to a person being unable to recognize familiar faces. Research concerning the condition has also contributed to the discussion of conscious versus unconscious processing. Russell Bauer worked with Patient LF, who was shown pictures of faces belonging to either family members or to famous people. In addition to LF inspecting the faces visually, his skin conductance (the extent to which his skin transmitted a small electric current) was also recorded. While the faces could not be

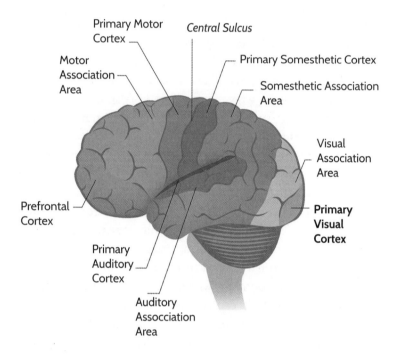

The Primary Visual Cortex is important for vision and is situated at the back of the brain. The condition blindsight is associated with damage to this area of the brain.

recognized visually, something very interesting occurred when five names were read out in association with each face. The names came from the same semantic category as the face which LF was currently inspecting, and there was a greater skin conductance response in association with the correct name rather than the incorrect names. This led Bauer to conclude that recognition had occurred, albeit this was not consciously visual, and he went on to argue that there are two brain pathways, one for overt or conscious recognition and one for covert, or unconscious, recognition. However, while this position has been accepted by some experts, others have disagreed, maintaining that face recognition proceeds by one route which simply cannot consciously recognize faces unless tested by a particularly sensitive means.

Another area of investigation has explored whether our choices and decisions to act are conscious or unconscious. Perhaps this seems a strange question for psychological investigation? Surely our deliberate actions are obviously the result of conscious decision making? Yet, this topic is far more important than it may seem at face value. It is not simply interesting because it tells us about how we decide: it goes beyond this, stretching to how we think of ourselves and, wider still, to society more broadly. We like to think that, even if it is not present in every aspect of living, we at least have some conscious choice in deciding our lot for some strands of life. Moreover, there are social and legal perspectives in deciding to act: Act A may stem from having made the moral and legally appropriate decision but Act B may not.

In the late 1990s, Daniel Wegner and Thalia Wheatley conducted an experiment from which they concluded that our assumption that we consciously cause actions is flawed. A number of participants took part in the study and they believed they were being tested in pairs. However, the other member of any pair was a confederate of the researchers. Both people put their fingers on a board beneath which was a computer mouse; this moved a cursor on a screen which showed pictures of small objects, such as a car and a swan. The cursor had to be stopped every 30 seconds or so, and at this point each person had to give a rating which indicated the extent to which the cursor had been stopped intentionally.

Both people wore headphones. Although the participant was under the impression that each person heard words and music, the confederate was actually hearing instructions to move the cursor. The words that the participant heard were intended to generate thoughts about the objects, such as 'car'. On particular occasions, the confederate stopped the cursor on certain designated objects. This was organized so that the participant heard the word which related to the object either 30 seconds, 5 seconds or 1 second prior to the cursor being stopped, or the word was heard 1 second after the cursor stopped.

The results revealed that when a word preceded a designated object 5 seconds or 1 second before the cursor was stopped by the confederate, participants considered this to be the product of their intention. That is, they wrongly concluded that their own conscious intention was responsible for the act of stopping the cursor. From this, the researchers contended that since the appearance of intention could be created, our experience of conscious intention stems from how we interpret causality. What actually mentally causes our acts is separate from this.

In later work, Wegner considered how the interpretation of causality operates. He did this by drawing on the *theory of apparent mental causation* and by discussing the three principles of priority, consistency and exclusivity in relation to switching on a light. Suppose that immediately prior to switching on a light you have the conscious thought about taking this action. This thought is consistent with the action and if there isn't anything or anyone else who could have been responsible for the light going on, you determine that it was you who caused the light to come on. Your mind has imputed causation to itself because it has drawn a causal connection between thought and action.

Despite maintaining that our experience of conscious intention stems from how we interpret causality, Wegner did not absolutely rule out any causal connection between conscious thought and action. Instead, he maintained such a connection may be present. What is important though, is that any such connection should be established via scientific investigation, since it is impossible to rely on our own minds to supply accurate evidence.

The two sets of work just discussed have not gone unchallenged, however. For instance, in the experiment described, when participants heard relevant words 5 seconds and 1 second before the cursor was stopped by the confederate, perceived intentionality was found to be 60 per cent or slightly higher. Perhaps this figure was so high because the study's design made it unnecessarily hard for participants to accurately determine what caused the cursor to stop? Perhaps in the real world we are more successful in determining whether we have consciously caused an action? It has been argued, too, that conscious intention is not always associated with something external to a person. Furthermore, other evidence signals that conscious decisions do affect conscious behaviour. Peter Gollwitzer and Paschal Sheeran have discussed evidence which shows that the likelihood of achieving a goal is increased when *if-then* planning is in place. Such a plan captures where, when and how the goal may be reached, while goal intentions, or instructions to oneself, to do x or achieve y are associated with a commitment to act.

Other examinations of conscious versus unconscious decision making have used neurological evidence. In the 1960s, Hans Kornhuber and Luder Deecke conducted research in which participants were asked to perform a simple action, such as moving a finger, hand or foot. The resultant brain activity was recorded via electrodes on a participant's scalp using electroencephalography (EEG). The researchers discovered that before the conscious, voluntary action was initiated, there was other, notably earlier brain activity, which was interpreted as being associated with preparation to make the action.

Drawing upon these results, Benjamin Libet explored the possibility of identifying the point at which the conscious

Electroencephalography (EEG) records brain activity through the use of electrodes attached to a person's scalp.

decision to act takes place. Of course, we typically think of ourselves as deciding to do something before we pursue the action. Following this assumption, if we consciously decide to do something, the decision should precede any brain activity associated with preparation to make an action. However, what Libet found was a different order: first there was readiness to act; then conscious awareness of the decision to act (self-reported from a visually inspected, specially adapted timing device); and finally, the act itself. This order suggested that, as readiness to act preceded conscious awareness of the decision to act, then the decision to act must be unconscious. Once again, though, this does not completely rule out consciousness affecting behaviour. This is because the time in between conscious awareness of the decision to act and subsequent movement allows for the movement to be prohibited before it takes place.

Libet's findings were fascinating but have attracted a number of criticisms. For example, some people were unhappy with the accuracy with which participants could subjectively report when their conscious awareness arose. Another problem came from the readiness to act on evidence being associated with the brain's supplementary motor area. This region is responsible for planning complex movements; consequently, the research may not be informative about any decision making which takes place before planning complex movements.

The question of conscious awareness and decision making was looked at again by Chun Siong Soon and colleagues. They used functional magnetic resonance imaging to identify which brain areas were involved before a conscious decision was made. Their experiment involved multiple occasions when participants had to make a decision about which response button to press. All button presses had to be made straight away, whenever participants felt the desire to push a button, and this was completed with either their left or right index finger. At the same time, a stream of letters was shown on a screen and the participant had to note which letter was on screen in association with button

Benjamin Libet.

pressing. Next, a new screen appeared with four choices and the participant indicated which of the four options corresponded with when the decision had been made. From analysis of the brain scan data, the researchers observed: (a) that decisions to act could be predicted by brain activity which occurred before conscious awareness of these decisions was present; and (b) that this brain activity was associated with a region in the prefrontal cortex (at the front of the brain's frontal lobe) and a region of the parietal cortex. From these results, it would appear that decision making is unconscious rather than conscious.

Yet, Soon and colleagues' research has been critiqued too. In fairness to the researchers, they deliberately designed a study which addressed problems in Libet's work but this in itself gave rise to difficulties. For instance, although a decision certainly had to be made between which buttons to press, this kind of relatively simple, specific decision –though necessary for the experiment – is nonetheless limited in telling us about decision making more generally. Life's decisions are often of a quite different character from button pressing; what was found in Soon et al.'s research, therefore, does not necessarily apply elsewhere. For example, some decision making is complex and far less immediate than selecting to push a button: hence, where greater complexity is present, it cannot be concluded that such decision making is unconscious in the same way.

Quite possibly, the reader is now left perplexed from back-and-forth arguments regarding conscious decision making. Where is the definitive answer as to whether we make conscious decisions to act? Furthermore, what are the potential implications for free will? Philosophy, psychology and neuroscience have all deliberated upon free will, but this does not mean that everybody has an agreed definition of what the concept constitutes! Leaving the issue of this definition aside, we are faced with a modern form of the dualist *mind/body problem* first raised by the French philosopher René Descartes (1596–1650).

René Descartes.

Julien Offray de la Mettrie.

Briefly, Descartes' position was that mind and body are different but interact in a small part of the brain called the pineal gland. He believed that the mind gained information from the bodily senses and could affect the body's actions, but that mental events were not physical events. This means that there is a division between consciousness (thought and will) and matter (including the brain). Later, the French physician and philosopher Julien Offray de la Mettrie (1709–1751) provided a materialistic understanding of the mind and brain. For him, mental processes were directly related to the brain and nervous system. From this perspective, mental experience and the brain are not divisible.

Of course, time has increased our knowledge such that the modern mind/brain debate is different from its forebears. Yet, the resolution favoured still depends on the perspective of the person addressing the issue. Let's look now at three of those perspectives.

Materialism equates the mind with physical brain processes. From this perspective, consciousness, the decisions we make and our experiences do not exist separately: they are all no more than the product of brain activity. *Epiphenomenalism*, on the other hand, allows for mind and brain to be different in the sense that a mental occurrence is not the same as a physical one. However, the mind cannot affect physical matter: mental events are a secondary occurrence resulting from what is taking place with the brain's nerve cells – that is, they are an epiphenomenon. In this way, consciousness and decisions are not causally related to action.

A third perspective comes from David Chalmers, who made use of the idea of a *philosophical zombie*. Such a creature is in all ways physically identical to a human and behaves like one but, critically, lacks consciousness. Taking this a step further, it can be contended that those arguments which maintain human consciousness does not exist lead to the conclusion that we are zombies. Yet, since we experience consciousness, any argument

ALIEN HAND SYNDROME

If you have ever seen Stanley Kubrick's film *Dr Strangelove*, starring Peter Sellers, you will be familiar with the way in which Dr Strangelove's right arm repeatedly moves upwards whilst his left hand attempts to prevent this. It is as though his arm is out of control, or anarchic.

Alien hand syndrome – also known as anarchic hand syndrome – is also referred to as Dr Strangelove syndrome due to its similarity to the behaviour of the eponymous character. It is a rare condition and it results from brain damage. To an observer, it appears as though the person's hand is being moved deliberately, but this is not so: the hand's movement occurs without wilful control.

All cases of alien hand syndrome are not the same: the affected hand moves differently according to the part of the brain where damage has occurred. In some people, the affected hand searches for objects in its vicinity, grasps

Those with alien hand syndrome exhibit behaviour similar to that displayed by this fictional character. A person's hand appears to move deliberately but actually moves without wilful control. Although called alien hand syndrome, the condition may affect an arm or a leg.

them or compulsively manipulates objects. In other people, there is intermanual conflict in which the hands appear to disagree with each other, the alien hand behaving in a manner which is at odds with the other hand. Having alien hand syndrome can affect daily life; intermanual conflict, for instance, may lead to distress because of the way in which the behaviour appears if the person is observed. For example, Sergio Della Sala described an incident where a woman was dining with others. When one of the other diners, her brother, ate an ice-cream the woman's affected hand grabbed it. Straight away, her other hand took action to rectify matters, but a disagreement between the hands ensued, which led to the ice-cream being deposited on the floor. From Della Sala's description of this incident and another one during the same meal, it is clear that the woman felt she had no control over her alien hand and found its behaviour embarrassing.

Another example of the behaviour of an alien hand comes from the BBC's *The Brain: A Secret History*. In this, Michael Moseley reported on the behaviour of Karen Byrne's alien hand, which resulted from a brain operation. Ms Byrne described how, if she lit a cigarette and left it on an ashtray, her alien hand would stub it out. Ms Byrne also found that one of her legs was sometimes affected, demonstrating that this syndrome, despite its name, is not limited to hands.

The syndrome has been used as evidence that it is the brain which produces our conscious, apparently deliberately decided upon, chosen behaviour. It is argued that: (a) if an action may appear to be deliberate but is not actually under volitional control and has resulted from brain functioning, then (b), it is equally plausible that decision making and volitional control in someone without an alien hand may also be the product of brain processes alone.

which refutes its existence must be able to account for this in physical terms. This does not mean that Chalmers denies that brain events are linked to consciousness, rather that consciousness cannot be reduced to what is occurring in the brain.

Which perspective do you prefer? While it would be too sweeping to assert that all scientists accept that consciousness originates in the brain, it would probably be fair to claim that most do so.

Key Points

- Consciousness is recognized to be: a state; experiences we can consciously access; and one's own subjective, private experience.
- Consciousness and wakefulness are not the same. In sleep we are conscious but not awake; someone in a vegetative state can exhibit wakefulness but lack consciousness.
- Some people in a vegetative state show evidence of consciousness. One patient's indicated conscious experience was similar to that of healthy individuals.
- Explaining cognitive functions and linking them to the brain is the easy problem of consciousness. The hard problem is explaining how the brain's physical processes yield subjective experience.
- Access consciousness involves what we can consciously report to ourselves and others; phenomenal consciousness is one's own subjective experience.
- Focused attention is conscious, but the completion of automatic tasks may not be conscious; inattentional blindness can occur in which an obvious item in vision is not perceived.
- Declarative memories are consciously remembered but nondeclarative memories are not consciously remembered. Declarative memory is associated with brain regions such as the hippocampus and the parahippocampal gyrus. Not all consciously experienced material can be reported.

- Blindsight has been used as evidence for visual awareness without consciousness; others have regarded the 'blind' part of blindsight as degraded vision.
- Prosopagnosia evidence has been used to argue for conscious and unconscious face recognition pathways. Others contend there is one route.
- Evidence for unconscious decision making exists but it is not without criticism.
- Whether consciousness equates to brain processes or not has been answered in different ways according to the materialistic, epiphenomenalistic and philosophical zombie perspectives.

Glossary

Accommodation Oculomotor depth cue; the eye's lens changes convexity to focus on objects.

Agnosia Results from brain damage leading to problems recognizing objects.

Aha moment When the solution to a problem suddenly comes to mind; associated with insight.

Algorithm The process of following a number of stages to solve a problem.

Alien hand syndrome A rare condition resulting from brain damage; the hand appears to move deliberately, but actually moves without volitional control.

Amnesia Temporary or permanent loss of memory due to brain damage. In **anterograde amnesia** memories cannot be accessed from after the brain damage; with **retrograde amnesia** memories cannot be accessed from before the brain damage.

Analogy In problem solving, where a current problem is deemed similar to a previous one which was resolved; the previous means of problem solving is applied to the current issue.

Aphasia An acquired language disorder; normal language and speech were present before a brain injury.

Attention The selection of external or internal information for processing.

Attenuation theory of attention An account of auditory attention. An attenuator acts like a filter, weakening all auditory input from attended messages.

Automatic processing This occurs when a task is so well practised or well learned that it requires little conscious processing.

Blindsight Results from damage to the primary visual cortex; a person reports blindness in all or part of the visual field but can still locate stimuli in the blind area.

Blind spot An anatomically blind area on the retina where the retina and optic nerve meet.

Binocular depth cues Visual cues which provide information concerning depth perception and which require both eyes.

Binocular disparity The different perspective or view of an object or scene provided by each eye.

Bruce and Young model An account of face processing.

Categorical syllogism Used as a test of reasoning. It consists of two premises and a conclusion: the task is to determine if the conclusion is true/false based on the premises.

Capacity of memory The size of a given kind of memory.

Coarticulation In speech, how the pronunciation of a phoneme is affected by the phoneme immediately before it and the phoneme immediately after.

Cocktail party problem The issue of how we focus attention on one speaker when surrounded by other conversations.

Cohort model An account of speech perception. In its original formulation, a heard word's early sound establishes the word-initial cohort, or that group of words which all begin with the same sound. As more sounds are heard in association with the original word, cohort words are eliminated which do not fit this sound pattern. Filtering not only occurs by using sound but also syntactic and semantic context.

Common ground The shared knowledge/understanding between speaker and audience.

Cones Cells in the eye's retina sensitive to detail and involved in colour perception.

Conjunction fallacy Occurs in decision making; where two pieces of information appearing together seem more likely to represent something or someone than one piece of information alone.

Consciousness Consciousness can be understood in different ways: (i) as a state; (ii) as experiences we can consciously access and report; (iii) one's own subjective, private experience.

Constraint-based models Accounts of parsing in which multiple factors constrain sentence interpretation, such as syntactic, semantic, context and plausibility information.

Controlled processing This occurs when conscious attention is needed to complete a task.

Cornea The curved, transparent part of the eye.

Declarative memory A form of long-term memory in which we consciously, or explicitly, remember information.

Dichotic listening An auditory research technique in which two different messages are presented simultaneously, one to the left ear and one to the right ear. In studies of attention, a participant is required to focus on one of the messages.

Dual task procedure Performing two tasks simultaneously.

Dual route cascaded model A computer model of reading which accounts for pronunciation of the written word in terms of two routes. These routes are the direct pathway, which is visual, and the indirect pathway which involves sounding out the word.

Duration of memory The period for which a given type of memory lasts.

Electroencephalography (EEG) The recording of brain activity using electrodes attached to the scalp.

Encoding The process by which information from the senses is put into a form that can be used by memory.

Encoding Specificity Theory A memory theory that argues that memory is better when there is a good overlap between information held in memory and the information available at retrieval.

Epiphenomenalism A perspective held on the mind/brain problem in which mind and brain are different in that mental events are not the same as physical events. The mind, however, does not affect physical matter; mental events result from what is taking place in the brain's nerve cells.

Episodic memory Long-term memory for where and when events and experiences have occurred.

Explicit learning The intentional lodging of information in memory.

Feature analysis theory Accounts which propose that object recognition occurs in terms of objects possessing distinctive features, or properties which characterize them.

Feature integration theory A visual search theory consisting of a preattentive parallel processing stage (which processes individual features) and a serial processing stage (which binds the features together).

Filter theory of attention An account of auditory attention. It proposes that a selective filter prevents too much information accessing short-term memory. Only attended information gets through the filter.

Fixations When reading, the eyes rest on or fixate certain words. This allows information to be taken in by the reader. Fixations usually occur on content words.

Flower and Hayes model of writing An account of how writing is produced which consists of three units: task environment, long-term memory and writing processes.

Fovea The small depression in the centre of the eye's retina.

Functional magnetic resonance imaging (fMRI) A type of scan that detects which regions of the brain are active in relation to different cognitive processes such as thinking, speaking, or performing tasks.

Garden path theory An account of parsing in which there are two stages. Initially, a sentence's grammatical structure is determined but if other non-syntactic sources of information reveal this interpretation to be incorrect, then further analysis takes place.

Geons Geons are the units, or easily distinguishable shapes, from which we build up the visual properties that characterize an object. There are approximately 36 such shapes, which include, for example, blocks, arcs and cones.

Gestalt theory of perception A theory of perception which proposed that we perceive an object by grouping together individual pieces of information into an organized whole. There are different laws of perceptual organization.

Gradient theory of attention An account of perception in which attention is organized in a gradient: attention is greatest at the point of focus; as distance from this point increases, attention decreases.

Guided search models Accounts of visual search; 6.0 is the most recent account and it details what guides attention during visual search.

Hayes model of writing An account of the process of writing which consists of the control level, process level and resource level.

Heuristic A 'rule of thumb' used to solve a problem.

If-then planning Planning which stipulates when, where and how a goal may be achieved.

Implicit learning The process of learning without conscious awareness that learning is occurring.

Inferences General knowledge, or knowledge of the world are used to elaborate on the meaning of speech or text beyond that which has been explicitly said or written.

Interactive spreading activation model A theory of word production in speech involving semantic, word and phoneme nodes.

Intonation The change in pitch in a person's speech.

Iris The coloured part of the eye.

Lemma A component of the WEAVER++ model; it represents a word's syntactic properties.

Lens The curved, transparent structure of the eye; it bends light to focus an image on the retina.

Levels of processing theory An account of long-term memory which proposes that deeper processing leads to better memory. Processing for meaning involves deep processing; processing based on perceptual information constitutes shallow processing.

Long-term memory The memory store that holds information for periods ranging from minutes to a lifetime.

McClelland and Rumelhart model A word recognition account consisting of feature, letter and word levels.

Marr and Nishihara model An account of object recognition in terms of the primal sketch, the 2½-D sketch and 3-D model representation.

Materialism A concept that equates the mind with physical brain processes.

Mind-body problem René Descartes' argument that mind and body are different: mental events are not physical events.

Monocular depth cues Visual cues which provide information regarding depth and which require only one eye.

Multimode theory of attention An account of selective attention which maintains selective attention can occur at different processing stages.

Neuron A nerve cell.

Nondeclarative memory A form of long-term memory in which we implicitly remember information.

Optic nerve The fibres that take information from the eye's retina to the brain.

Optic disc The part of the eye where the retina and optic nerve meet; see also *blind spot*.

Opponent process theory An account of colour perception which proposes that colour is perceived through opposing pairs of processes: blue-yellow, red-green, black-white.

Parsing The analysis of sentences for syntactic structure.

Philosophical zombie A creature identical to humans except that it lacks consciousness.

Prägnanz, law of A Gestalt principle stating that when we are presented with an object or shape our brain interprets it in the easiest form possible.

Priming Behaviour is primed when the current behaviour toward a stimulus is affected by previous experience of the same or similar stimulus.

Procedural memory Long-term memory for skills developed through repetition.

Prosody The emphasis, intonation and rhythm in speech.

Prosopagnosia, acquired A disorder of face recognition caused by brain damage. Previously intact recognition of familiar faces is now impaired.

Prosopagnosia, developmental A disorder of face recognition that is not caused by brain damage; a deficit in familiar face recognition has always been present.

Pupil The black opening in the iris.

Primary visual cortex Information from the retina travels via the optic nerve to this region which is located at the back of the brain. It is one of a number of brain areas responsible for visual processing.

Propositional/conditional reasoning Reasoning based on propositional calculus. A propositional reasoning task consists of (i) antecedent and consequent propositions; (ii) affirmation or denial of one of the propositions; (iii) a conclusion which is either valid or invalid.

Recognition by components theory An account of how we recognize objects by building their shape from *geons*.

Regression In reading, a backward saccades.

Retina The eye's light-sensitive lining.

Retrieval The accessing of stored material from memory; this can be by **recognition**, (identifying that a stimulus has been encountered before), or **recall** (searching through memory for the information).

Rhythm in speech The timing of what is said.

Rods Retina cells which help us see in low light and perceive movement in peripheral vision.

Root morpheme exchange error A slip of the tongue in which the roots of two words exchange, but inflections such as -ed, -s etc., stay in place.

Saccades The rapid jumps of the eyes that are made when reading.

Schema A single unit of knowledge stored in long-term, semantic memory and which holds multiple pieces of information in an organized framework or structure.

Script A form of schema which allows us to remember the sequence of events in a setting.

Sensory memory The very brief storage of information detected by the senses.

Semantic memory Long-term memory for general knowledge about the world.

Short-term memory Memory that is only held for seconds. See *working memory.*

Shadowing Identical to *dichotic listening,* but where the message must be repeated verbatim.

Shape constancy The way in which the perceptual system allows for changes in an object's retinal image shape. When observed from different perspectives, an object's retinal image shape changes, yet we do not perceive the object as having changed shape.

Size constancy The way in which the perceptual system allows for increases/decreases in distance when perceiving size. Changes in distance alter the size of an object on the retina, yet we perceive its size to be unchanged.

Spoonerism A speech error involving the reversal of two consonant or two vowel phonemes.

Spotlight theory of attention An account of focused attention. It proposes that focused visual attention operates like a mental spotlight; it shines on what is being attended so that this information receives priority processing.

Storage The retention of an item in memory.

Stress in speech The emphasis applied to what is said.

Trichromatic theory An account of colour perception in terms of the retina possessing red, blue and green *cones.*

Temporally coherent sound modulations A speaker's changes in loudness and pitch which bind sounds together.

Template theory An early account of object recognition. It proposed objects that are recognized by comparing the currently viewed object with patterns stored in memory.

Texture-tiling model An account of visual search; the ease of visual search relates to the level of peripheral information in the visual field.

Unilateral spatial neglect A condition in which brain damage leads to a person being unable to pay attention to one half of space.

Unrestricted race model An account of parsing. It contends that all relevant information is used to parse a sentence. Ambiguous sentences generate more than one potential structure and whichever structure assembled first is the one selected.

Vegetative state A condition arising from severe brain damage and where the person exhibits wakefulness and a lack of consciousness.

Visual perception The application of meaning to visual sensation.

Visual search A perceptual task that requires attention: a target object must be located among other objects. In experimental visual search, the characteristics of the target and other objects (distractors) are manipulated.

Visual sensation Results from electrochemical changes occurring in neurons as they respond to information in the visual environment.

Wason selection task A test of deductive reasoning that uses four cards.

Weaver++ An account of speech production. It consists of concept, lemma and word-form levels.

Word exchange errors A speech error in which the positions of two words are swapped within a clause.

Working memory The term now used for short-term memory.

Working memory model An account of working memory comprising the central executive, phonological loop, visuo-spatial sketchpad and episodic buffer.

Zoom lens theory of attention An extension of the *spotlight approach*. The area of focused attention increases or decreases in a manner similar to a camera's zoom lens.

Index

Picture credits

t = top, b = bottom

Alamy: 59, 219

Getty Images: 174, 214

National Library of Medicine, USA: 99

Paul Oakley: 203

Princeton: 95

Reuters: 98

Science Photo Library: 57

Shutterstock: 16, 20, 22, 24, 26, 29 (x2), 33 (x3), 36, 42, 45, 48, 52, 64, 69, 71, 72, 81, 89, 90, 102, 105, 110, 111, 115, 122, 132 (x3), 133, 141, 143, 148, 150 (x2), 158, 163b, 170, 180 (x3), 182, 185, 190, 192, 201, 206, 208, 212

Wikimedia Commons: 76, 96, 131, 160 (x2), 163t, 178, 198, 216, 217